Sh*t
My
Dad
Says

Sh*t
My
Dad
Says

Justin Halpern

it
*it***books**
AN IMPRINT OF HARPERCOLLINS*PUBLISHERS*

The names and identifying characteristics of some of the individuals featured throughout this book have been changed to protect their privacy. Any resemblance to actual persons, living or dead, is purely coincidental.

HarperCollins books may be purchased for educational, business, or sales promotional use. For information please write: Special Markets Department, HarperCollins Publishers, 10 East 53rd Street, New York, NY 10022.

FIRST EDITION

Designed by Ashley Halsey

Library of Congress Cataloging-in-Publication Data has been applied for.

ISBN 978-0-06-199270-4

11 12 13 14   OV/RRD   30 29 28 27 26 25

For my dad, mom, Dan, Evan, José, and Amanda
Thank you for all your love and support

Introduction

"All I ask is that you pick up your shit so you don't leave your bedroom looking like it was used for a gang bang. Also, sorry that your girlfriend dumped you."

When I was twenty-eight years old, I lived in Los Angeles and was in the third year of a long-distance relationship with my girlfriend, who lived in San Diego. Most Fridays I'd sit in traffic for three and a half hours as my 1999 Ford Ranger crawled 126 miles down the I-5 to San Diego. Every once in a while my car would decide to shut off its engine. Meanwhile, its radio was busted, so I only got one station, whose playlist seemed limited to songs from the burgeoning rapper Flo Rida. There's nothing like merging onto a freeway only to have your engine stop, steering wheel lock, and a deejay scream, "And here's MY MAN, Flo Rida, with his new hit 'Right Round'! Let's get this party started!"

In short, doing the long-distance thing was wearing on me. So when I received a job offer in May 2009 from Maxim.com that would allow me to work from anywhere, I jumped at the opportunity. I could move down to San Diego and live with my girlfriend. The only hitch in my plan was that my girlfriend was not as excited as I was. And by "not as excited," I mean to say that when I showed up at her doorstep to deliver the good news in person, she broke up with me.

Driving away from her house, I realized that not only was I now single, I had no place to live since I had already told my landlord in Los Angeles that I was terminating my lease at the end of the month. Then my engine shut off. As I sat in my car vigorously trying to restart it, it dawned on me that the only people I knew in San Diego who might have room for me were my parents. My stomach started to tense up as I turned the key back and forth in the ignition. It also dawned on me that the family barbecuing on the deck of the house in front of which my car had stalled just might think I was a perv who'd pulled over to pleasure himself. Luckily my car started up within a minute and I sped off for my parents' house.

The reason I had become so nervous so quickly was because asking my father for a favor is like arguing a case in front of the Supreme Court: You have to lay out the facts clearly, organize them into an argument, and cite precedents set in previous cases. Shortly after showing up unannounced at my parents' modest three-bedroom house in our San Diego suburb, Point Loma, I was pleading my case before my parents in the living room. I cited *My Dad v. My Brother Daniel Halpern,* which led to my brother Dan living at home when he was twenty-nine and going through a "transitional phase." About halfway through my argument, my dad cut me off.

"It's fine. Jesus, you didn't have to go through that whole bullshit song and dance. You know you can stay here. All I ask is that you pick up your shit so you don't leave your bedroom looking like it was used for a gang bang," he said. "Also, sorry that your girlfriend dumped you."

The last time I had lived at home was ten years prior, during my sophomore year at San Diego State University. At the time, both my parents worked—my mother, as a lawyer for a nonprofit; and my father, in nuclear medicine at the University of California–San Diego—so I didn't see them very often. Ten years later, my mom was still working full-time, but my seventy-three-year-old dad had retired and was around the house. All. Day. Long.

After my first night back home, I crawled out of bed at around 8:30 A.M. and set up my "office" (read: my laptop) in the living room, where my dad was watching TV, to begin writing my first column. Michael Jackson had just died, and I was working on a comic portraying Jesus overlooking the pedophile charges against Michael Jackson and letting him into Heaven anyway, because he was such a fan of the King of Pop. (My editor later pointed out that it should have been Saint Peter ushering M.J. through the gates of Heaven, but that's beside the point.) My dad had a hard time understanding that someone sitting in his pajamas and searching through Google images for silly pictures of Jesus Christ was working. So he treated me like I wasn't.

"Why the fuck is Wolf Blitzer talking to me about Michael Jackson?" he barked. "The president is in fucking Russia trying to get those sons of bitches to stop with the nukes, and he's talking to me about Michael Jackson? Fuck you, Wolf Blitzer!"

Every so often throughout the rest of the day, my dad would get fired up about something, bound into the living room from the kitchen or front yard or wherever he'd been, and shout something like, "Are you putting ketchup on that hamburger I made you?"

"Yeah, why?"

"Why? What the fuck do you mean, *why*? That's a gourmet hamburger. This ain't some horseshit you cook. I spent time on that. Next time, I make shit for you."

It was good to be home.

For as long as I've known him, my father has been a blunt individual. When I was little, I mostly felt terrified of him, so I couldn't appreciate that I was dealing with the least passive-aggressive human being on the planet. Now, as an adult, all day long I dealt with people—friends, coworkers, relatives—who never really said what they were thinking. The more time I spent with my dad in those first couple months back home, the more grateful I started to feel for the mixture of honesty and insanity that characterized his comments and personality.

One day I was on a walk with him and my dog, Angus, who was sniffing around in a bush outside a neighbor's house. My dad turned to me and said, "Look at the dog's asshole."

"What? Why?"

"You can tell by the dilation of his asshole that he's going to shit soon. See. There it goes."

It was at that moment, as my dog emptied his bowels in my neighbor's yard and my dad stood there proudly watching his prediction come true, that I realized how wise, even prophetic, he really is.

I took that quote and posted it as my instant messenger away status that evening. And every day after that, I'd take one funny remark my dad said and use it to update my status. When one of my friends suggested I create a Twitter page to keep a record of all the crazy things that come out of his mouth, I started "Shit My Dad Says." For about a week, I had only a handful of followers—a couple friends who knew my dad and thought he was a character. Then one day I woke up to find that a thousand people were following me. The next day, ten thousand. Then fifty thousand. Then one hundred, two hundred, three hundred thousand, and suddenly a picture of my dad's face and his quotes were popping up everywhere. Literary agents were calling, wanting to represent me; TV producers were inviting me onto their shows; and reporters were asking for interviews.

My first thought was: This is not good. The emotion that followed can only be described as sheer panic.

To illustrate how much my father hates any kind of public attention, let me share his opinion of contestants who compete on *Jeopardy!* My dad's a well-read, educated guy, and one evening when I was watching *Jeopardy!* he strolled into the living room and correctly answered every question Alex Trebek posed. "Dad, you should totally go on *Jeopardy!*," I said.

"Are you fucking kidding me? Look at those people. They have no fucking respect for themselves. No dignity. Going on a reality show like that, it sickens me."

I knew I had to tell my dad that I had been posting his quotes and quips online and now had publishers and TV studios interested in adaptations of the material. But before I did, I figured I'd call my oldest brother, Dan, with the hope that he would tell me I was blowing the situation out of proportion and that our dad would be fine with it.

"Holy shit, you did what?" Dan said to me, in between giant belly laughs. "Dude, Dad is going to—I don't even know what Dad's going to do. You better be prepared to leave his house. Like, if I were you, I'd pack up my stuff beforehand, fugitive-style. Only important belongings that can be carried with one arm."

I decided to take a walk around the block and gather my thoughts before I confronted my father. A walk around the block turned into a few miles around the block, and as I was finally heading back toward the house an hour later, I spotted him sitting on our front porch looking like he was in a good mood. I figured it was now or never.

"Hey, Dad, I have to tell you something . . . weird," I said, tentatively sidling up next to him on a nearby deck chair.

"You have to tell me something weird, huh? What is weird that you have to tell me?" he replied.

"So, there's this thing called Twitter," I said.

"I know what Twitter is, goddamn it. You talk to me like I don't know what shit is. I know what it is. You have to start up the Internet to get on Twitter," he said, making the universal sign for turning a key in the ignition when he said the words "start up the Internet."

I laid it all out there: the Twitter page, the hundreds of thousands of followers, the news articles, the book publishers, the TV producers, all of it. He sat quietly and listened. Then he laughed, stood up, ironing out his pants with his hands, and said, "Have you seen my cell phone? Can you call it? I can't find it."

"So you're . . . cool with all this? You're cool with me writing a book, the quotes, everything?" I asked.

"What do I give a fuck? I don't care what people think of me. Publish whatever you want. I just got two rules: I'm not talking to anyone, and whatever money you get, keep. I got my own fucking money. I don't need yours," he said. "Now, call my cell phone, goddamn it."

Sh*t
My
Dad
Says

Never Assume That Which You Do Not Know

"Well, what the fuck makes you think Grandpa wants to sleep in the same room as you?"

In the summer of 1987, when I was six years old, my cousin got married on a farm in Washington state. My family lived in San Diego, and my dad decided there was no way he was paying a thousand dollars for himself, my mother, my two brothers, and me to fly up the coast.

"Why am I going to pay two hundred dollars so a six-year-old can see a wedding?" he said to my mother. "You think that's a moment Justin cares about? Two years ago he was still shitting in his pants. If everyone has to go, we're driving."

And so we did. I squished in between my two older brothers—Dan, who was sixteen at the time, and Evan, fourteen and gangly—in the backseat of our '82 Thunderbird. My mom rode shotgun, and my dad took the wheel as we began the 1,800-mile trip up to Washington. We made it about four miles before my brothers and I started tormenting one another, which mostly consisted of them hitting me and saying stuff like, "How come you're sitting like a gay? I bet it's 'cause you're a gay." My dad dramatically swerved off to the side of the road, tires squealing in our wake, and whipped his head around to the three of us.

"You listen to me. I'm not going to deal with any of your bullshit, understand? We will all behave like human fucking beings."

But we didn't. There was no way we could have. This wasn't a situation that "human fucking beings" were built for. We were five people, three of us males under the age of seventeen, sitting a half-inch from one another for sixteen hours a day as the seemingly endless highway inched by. This was not a normal sightseeing family vacation. It was like we were running from the law: We drove all day and all night, growing more and more sweaty and on edge by the hour, with my dad regularly making desperate comments to himself like, "We just gotta fucking get there, it can't be that much farther."

More than a day and a half later, after twenty-four hours of driving, we made it to Olympia, Washington, where we met our extended family in the lobby of a hotel. In total, about sixty of us Halperns were staying there, including my ninety-year-old grandpa, my dad's father. A quiet but tough guy, he hated when people made a big deal about him. He had run a tobacco farm in Kentucky until he was seventy-five, and just because he was older now, he wasn't about to start accepting help where, in his opinion, it wasn't necessary.

My family had reserved a block of hotel rooms, each to be shared by two people, but no one had been assigned to a specific room yet. My brothers quickly decided they would share a room with each other, and my mom and dad would obviously share one, which left me without a partner. For some reason, all my adult relatives thought "it would just be so cute" if I shared a room with Grandpa. Grandpa had stayed with us in San Diego before, and I remembered that he always kept a bottle of Wild Turkey in his room, and would clandestinely take a swig from time to time. Once when my brother Dan caught him in the act, Grandpa shouted "You got me!" and then laughed hysterically. I also remembered that he needed help getting out of bed but got really angry when anyone tried to assist him. There was no way I wanted to share a room with Grandpa, but I kept my concerns to myself because I figured my family would hate me for being so unfriendly.

So, like any six-year-old who doesn't want to do something, I faked being sick, which attracted a lot more attention to me. Upon hearing that I wasn't feeling well, my aunts hurried me down the carpeted hallway to my parents' room and burst into it like it was an episode of *ER*.

"Okay, everyone calm down, goddamn it. Now leave, so I can check out the boy," my dad shouted. My aunts cleared out, leaving the two of us alone. He looked me in the eye and felt my forehead with his hand.

"You say you're sick, huh? Well, it looks like you've come down with a case of bullshit. You ain't sick. What's the problem here? We just drove a goddamned continent, and I'm tired. Spit it out."

"Everybody wants me to share a room with Grandpa, but I don't want to," I replied.

"Well, what the fuck makes you think Grandpa wants to sleep in the same room as you?"

I hadn't thought about that. "I don't know."

"Well, let's go ask him."

We walked down the hallway to the room Grandpa had staked out. He was busy getting ready for bed.

"Look here, Dad. Justin doesn't want to share a room with you. What do you think about that?"

I cowered behind my dad's leg, as he kept shoving me away toward my grandfather to make me face him. Grandpa looked me in the eye for a second.

"Well, I don't want to share a room with him, neither. I want my own room," he said.

My dad turned and looked at me like he had just uncovered the missing clue in a murder case. "There you have it," he said. "Apparently you're no goddamned peach, either."

On Toilet Training

"You are four years old. You have to shit in the toilet. This is not one of those negotiations where we'll go back and forth and find a middle ground. This ends with you shitting in a toilet."

On My First Day of Kindergarten

"You thought it was hard? If kindergarten is busting your ass, I got some bad news for you about the rest of life."

On Accidents

"I don't give a shit how it happened, the window is broken. . . . Wait, why is there syrup everywhere? Okay, you know what? Now I give a shit how it happened. Let's hear it."

On My Seventh Birthday Party

"No, you can't have a bouncy house at your birthday party. . . . What do you mean why? Have you ever thought to yourself, where would I put a goddamned bouncy house in our backyard? . . . Yeah, that's right, that's the kind of shit I think about, that you just think magically appears."

On Talking to Strangers

"Listen up, if someone is being nice to you, and you don't know them, run away. No one is nice to you just to be nice to you, and if they are, well, they can go take their pleasant ass somewhere else."

On Table Manners

"Jesus Christ, can we have one dinner where you don't spill something? . . . No, Joni, he *does* do it on purpose, because if he doesn't, that means he's just mentally handicapped, and none of the tests showed that."

On Crying

"I had no problem with you crying. My only concern was with the snot that was coming out of your nose. Where does that go? On your hands, your shirt? That's no good. Oh, Jesus, don't start crying."

On Spending the Night at a Friend's House for the First Time

"Try not to piss yourself."

On Being Teased

"So he called you a homo. Big deal. There's nothing wrong with being a homosexual. . . . No, I'm not saying you're a homosexual. Jesus Christ. Now I'm starting to see why this kid was giving you shit."

On Feeling Comfortable in One's Own Skin

"It's my house. I'll wear clothes when I want to wear clothes, and I'll be naked when I want to be naked. The fact that your friends are coming over shortly is inconsequential to that—aka I don't give a shit."

A Man's House
Is His House

"This is my house, goddamn it! I gotta defend MY house!"

When I was seven years old, my dad invited me into his bedroom to show me his Mossberg shotgun. "Here's the trigger, here's the loading mechanism, here's the sight so you can see whatever the fuck you're shooting, and here's how you hold it," he said, cradling the gun. "Now, don't ever fucking touch it."

The reason that my dad kept a shotgun on top of the cabinet above his bed was because he was convinced that we were always just about to be robbed. "We have a lot of shit in this house. People want that shit. I do not want them to get our shit. Make sense?" It did, but to my dad, anyone making noise inside our house after 1:00 A.M. was likely a burglar. I never understood where his anxiety came from, because we lived in a suburb. I once asked him about it, and he responded simply, "I came from a different time."

"What time was that, Dad?"

"I don't fucking know, a different one. Jesus, stop asking me questions and just be thankful I give a shit."

Despite his ever-present fear of burglars, my father likes to get comfy when he goes to bed. Meaning that he always sleeps naked. And when he's naked, he looks like something that pops up from behind a bush in a Jim Henson film and starts singing: superhairy, with eyebrows that defy gravity.

One night shortly after he showed me his shotgun, my dad awoke to hear a rumbling in the kitchen at about 1:45 A.M. He immediately grabbed his gun from over the bed, told my mom to stay put, and walked bare-ass naked toward the noise, gun out in front, hand on the trigger. I woke up when I heard him clomp past my door, and peeped my head out of my bedroom just in time to see him get down on all fours with his shotgun and army-crawl toward the door that led to the kitchen. My dad stopped in the middle of the hallway, then aimed his shotgun at the closed door and yelled, "Come through this door, and I'll fucking kill you!"

Inside the kitchen was my mom's sister, Aunt Jeanne, who was staying with us, and, unaware of the 1:00 A.M. burglar rule, had decided to fix herself a late-night snack. Upon hearing his threat, she opened the door, spotted my father naked on the floor, with a shotgun pointed at her and his exposed rear reflecting the light from the kitchen. She ran past him into her room and slammed the door. My dad assumed she was just afraid of the burglar and remained agitated.

Oblivious to what was going on outside her bedroom, my mom called 911. "Sam! The police are on the way! Put your gun down and your clothes on!" she hollered from the other side of the house.

"Fuck that, I ain't doing either! This is my house, goddamn it! I gotta defend MY house!" he yelled back.

The police finally showed up, determined that there had been no foul play, and encouraged my father to put his clothes on and disarm himself.

The next morning my brothers, my parents, and I sat silently at the breakfast table. When my aunt came out of her room for the first time since she had retreated from my naked, gun-wielding father, she was not talkative, either. Just in case I hadn't realized what had happened, my brother Dan leaned over and whispered to me, "She saw Dad's wiener, then he tried to kill her."

My dad turned to us and said in a serious tone, "I guess I should fill you in on what happened last night. No one broke into the house. BUT, remember, a man's house is his house."

He took one last bite of Grape-Nuts and chirped, "Okay, gotta go to work."

On Chivalry

"Give your mother the front seat. . . . I don't give a shit if she said you could have it, that's what she's supposed to do, and you're supposed to say, 'No, I insist.' You think I'm gonna drive around with my wife in the backseat and a nine-year-old in the front? You're a crazy son of a bitch."

On Candy

"Jesus Christ, one fucking Snickers bar, and you're running around like your asshole is on fire. Okay, outside you go. Don't come back in until you're ready to sleep or shit."

On Going Away to Camp

"Relax, it'll be fine. You'll build fires, set up tents, sleep outside, it'll be fun. . . . Oh, it's basketball camp? Huh. Well, cross out that shit I said you were gonna do and just replace it with 'play basketball,' I guess."

On Summer Vacation

"Watching TV all day is not an option. If this were *Let's Make a Deal,* that would not be behind one of the doors to choose from."

On Off-Limits Zones in Hide-and-Go-Seek

"What the fuck are you doing in my closet? Don't shush me, it's my fucking closet."

On Sportsmanship

"You pitched a great game, you really did. I'm proud of you. Unfortunately, your team is shitty. . . . No, you can't go getting mad at people because they're shitty. Life will get mad at them, don't worry."

On Getting in Trouble at School

"Why would you throw a ball in someone's face? . . . Huh. That's a pretty good reason. Well, I can't do much about your teacher being pissed, but me and you are good."

On Making a Christmas List

"You ranked the twenty-five presents you want, in order of how much you want them? Are you insane? I said tell me what you want for Christmas, not make a fucking college football poll."

On Waterslides

"You go on ahead. I'd rather not be shot out of a tube into a pool filled with a bunch of nine-year-olds' urine."

On Packing My Own Lunch

"You have to pack a sandwich. It can't just be cookies and bullshit. . . . No, I said if you packed it yourself, you could pack it how you want it, not pack it like a moron."

It's Important to Behave Oneself

"Fucking hell! All I asked, goddamn it, was that you sit still for a couple hours while I lectured on thyroid cancer!"

When I turned ten, my mom decided she wanted to go to law school. My dad was supportive of her career goals, even though they meant that he'd have to assume more of the responsibility of watching me.

"Me and you are gonna be spending more time together, but a lot of that time, I'm going to be working, and I'm going to need you to not talk and entertain yourself," he explained to me after my mother showed us her first semester's class schedule.

Like a lot of kids, I never really understood what my dad did for a living. All I knew was that it was called "nuclear medicine" and that he often came home from work tired and irritable. On a couple weekday afternoons before my mom went back to school for her law degree, she'd been unable to watch me and had dropped me off at the V.A., which was one of the hospitals my dad worked at. On each occasion, he'd come out of his office to greet me, hand me a Snickers bar from his pocket, then walk me into a spare, unoccupied office near his.

"I got a couple more hours of work, so, you know, just sit here for a bit," he'd say.

Inevitably, I'd try to get him to nail down a specific time frame. "Is two hours the longest I'll be here, or could it be longer?" I'd ask.

"I don't know, son, I'm not a fucking psychic. I promise you as soon as I'm done, we'll leave, and I'll buy you an ice cream."

Then he'd look around the office and find a magazine for me to read.

"Here, you can take a look at the *New England Journal of Medicine*. Lots of interesting stuff in there."

Once my mom got into the thick of her law school classes, my dad had to pick up more and more of her slack, and I spent frequent afternoons counting down the minutes until he and I could leave the hospital and head home. Weekends were usually fine, because I could go to a friend's house, but on one particular weekend my mom was busy preparing for a test, and my dad had to give a speech to a hundred doctors, and none of my friends or family could watch me.

"I think we can just leave him at the house. He'll be fine," my dad said to my mom.

"Sam, I'm not leaving him alone here by himself. He's ten," my mom replied.

"Fine, I'll take him, goddamn it."

I hopped into my dad's Oldsmobile and we headed up to the University of California–San Diego campus. He didn't say much as he was driving, but I could see he was annoyed. As we pulled up to the lecture hall, he turned to me and said, "I need you to be well be-haved, you understand? No bullshit."

"Can I draw stuff?" I asked.

"What does that mean? What would you draw? I don't want one of these guys walking up to you and you're drawing two dogs fucking or something. I gotta be professional here."

"I don't know how to draw that. I just draw airplanes," I said.

He opened up his black leather briefcase, grabbed a piece of lined notepad paper and a multicolored pen, and handed them to me. We got out of the car, and I followed him through the glass doors of a big university building and through the lobby to a lecture hall that was filled with doctors, all of whom seemed to know my dad. He intro-duced me to a few people and then took me over to the back row of chairs that stood about a hundred feet from the stage and podium at the front of the room.

"Okay, here's your seat. Here's a king-size Snickers. If you start to get sleepy, eat it," he said, giving me a candy bar the size of my forearm. "All right. I gotta go do my shit."

The doctors filed into the rows, took their seats, and the confer-ence started. My dad sat up onstage while some other guy with a giant forehead starting talking. About two minutes in, I had already devoured the entire Snickers bar and was beginning to feel the ef-fects of the thirty-five grams of sugar that were making their way into my bloodstream. Every minute of the lecture felt like an hour. I couldn't sit still and decided I needed to get on the ground so I could blow off some steam where nobody could see me. I crawled down onto the floor right as I heard the man speaking introduce my dad.

I popped my head up, and as I did, I saw him, a hundred feet away, staring at me intensely, as if he had been tracking me the entire time. I quickly ducked back down behind the chairs in front of me.

As I crouched on the ground, I realized that I could fit in between the legs of the chairs, and that each row contained a few chairs that were empty. I thought it would be a really fun game—and no bother to anyone—if I crawled on my hands and knees, from my row in the back, to the front row, using the empty chairs to advance forward. I carefully began my journey, crawling laterally, underneath the un-suspecting rears of oncologist after oncologist, until I reached an open chair in the row in front, and then I'd move forward a row. It was like a real-life game of Frogger. And I was doing pretty well until I'd advanced seven rows forward and realized there were no more open chairs in front of me. But when I turned around to go back, I saw that someone had filled in the one empty chair in the row behind me. I was stuck.

The sound of my dad's voice over the speaker system sounded like the voice of God, if God were talking about molecular biology. I decided my only shot at getting back to my seat was to crawl over the feet of the fifteen or so doctors who sat between me and the aisle, where I figured I could get really low to the ground and slither back to my chair without my dad spotting me. Unfortunately the doctors didn't share my determination to hide my antics and did not play along as if nothing was happening. Instead, they stood up one by one as I tried to crawl past, whispering expressions of irritation to one another. And although I was on the ground and couldn't see any-thing, I heard my dad abruptly stop speaking. He knew something was up. I froze. When he started speaking again, I thought I was in the clear and forged ahead—until I accidentally smashed my knee into the loafer of a bearded guy sitting two seats from the aisle.

"Ah—God—this is ridiculous!" he huffed through his whiskers.

My dad stopped speaking again. I slowly crawled out past the last chair, then turned my head toward the stage, where he was staring right at me, along with everyone else.

The lecture hall was completely silent as I stood up, pretending nothing at all had happened, and walked back to my seat, averting my eyes from the room full of disbelieving gazes. I sat back down in my chair. After a couple moments, my dad began speaking again. His face was bright red and looked like a dodgeball with a furious frown and angry eyebrows. Suddenly his lecture on thyroid cancer had the same inflection as a coach tearing his football team a new one at halftime.

My dad ended his talk quickly and rushed through answering a couple of questions. As the audience applauded, he hopped down off the stage, choosing not to use the stairs. He made a beeline toward me, ignoring all the doctors who stood up to chat or compliment his lecture. He picked me up by my belt from the back of my pants like he was holding a six-pack of beer, pushed through the doors to the lobby, and then outside into the light. He carried me like that all the way to the car, opened the door, and tossed me in the front seat. He got in the driver's seat, where he took a few deep breaths, the veins in his neck bulging with anger. Then he turned to me and through clenched teeth yelled, "Fucking hell! All I asked, goddamn it, was that you sit still for a couple hours while I lectured on thyroid cancer!" He peeled out of the parking lot and drove us home in complete silence.

When we arrived at our house, he opened the front door. I was standing next to him on the doormat when he turned to me and calmly said, "Listen, that was not a place where a kid should have been. I get that. But I'm going to go inside this house, and you are not. You are going to play outside of this house, because right now, my fucking head is going to explode." Then he closed the door, and I stood outside, not sure what to do. From inside the house, I heard an echoing scream, "FUUUUUUUUUUUCCCCCCCCCCCCCCK!!!!!"

About an hour and a half later, he poked his head out the back door. I was sitting in the grass in our backyard.

"You can come on in if you want," he said. "Also, wash your hands before you touch stuff. That conference hall floor smelled like dog shit and you were crawling around like a little monkey on it."

On Finding Out I Didn't Make the Little League All-Star Team

"This is bullshit. All the coaches just put their kids on the team. That shit bag's son isn't worthy of carrying your jock strap. . . . You don't wear a jock strap? What the hell is wrong with you, son?"

On Dropping Me Off at School

"Your friends' parents drive like assholes. Tell them it's an elementary school parking lot, not downtown fucking Manhattan."

On Getting a Dog

"Who's going to take care of it? You? . . . Son, you came in the house yesterday with shit on your hands. Human shit. I don't know how that happened, but if someone has shit on their hands, it's an indicator that maybe the whole responsibility thing isn't for them."

On Showering with Regularity

"You're ten years old now, you have to take a shower every day. . . . I don't give a shit if you hate it. People hate smelly fuckers. I will not have a smelly fucker for a son."

On LEGOs

"Listen, I don't want to stifle your creativity, but that thing you built there, it looks like a pile of shit."

On Bring-Your-Dad-to-School Day

"Who are all these fucking parents who can take a day off? If I'm taking a day off, I ain't gonna spend it sitting at some tiny desk with a bunch of eleven-year-olds."

On My Sixth-Grade Parent-Teacher Conference

"I don't think that teacher likes you, so I don't like her. You ding off more shit than a pinball, but goddamn it, you're a good kid. She can go fuck herself."

On My First School Dance

"Are you wearing perfume? . . . Son, there ain't any cologne in this house, only your mother's perfume. I know that scent, and let me tell you, it's disturbing to smell your wife on your thirteen-year-old son."

On Being Afraid to Use the Elementary School Bathrooms to Defecate

"Son, you're complaining to the wrong man. I can shit anywhere, at any time. It's one of my finer qualities. Some might say my finest."

On My Last-Place Finish in the 50-Yard Dash During Little League Tryouts

"It kinda looked like you were being attacked by a bunch of bees or something. Then when I saw the fat kid with the watch who was timing you start laughing. . . . Well, I'll just say it's never a good sign when a fat kid laughs at you."

Do Not Be a Goddamned Liar

"You have shamed the entire scientific community. Fucking Einstein, everybody."

I've never been very good at math or science. I enjoyed the stories embedded in history and literature but lost interest when it came to periodic functions and the table of elements. So in sixth grade, when each member of my class was responsible for creating an experiment to show at the school's science fair in late April, I felt about as excited as I'd feel today if I were told I had to attend a live reenactment of the entire first season of *Grey's Anatomy*. My dad, on the other hand, was thrilled. He had spent the past twenty-five years performing medical and scientific research.

"Now you can get a glimpse into what my life is like every goddamned day," he told me the night I received my assignment. "I'm going to be on your ass every step of the way. You will have the greatest science experiment that school has ever seen, or you will fucking die trying."

"Will you do it with me?" I pleaded.

"What? No, I already do it all the goddamned day on my own. That's what I just told you."

He took a seat on our living room couch and motioned for me to take a seat next to him.

"Now, experiments start with a question. What do you want to know?"

I thought about it for a few seconds.

"I think the dog is cool," I said, motioning toward Brownie, our five-year-old chocolate Lab mix.

"What? What the hell does that mean? That's not a fucking question."

"What if I said: Do people think the dog is cool?"

"Jesus fucking Christ," he said, rubbing his temples. "Think of a question like Do larger objects fall faster than smaller ones? Something like that."

"Okay. Well, can the question be something about the dog?"

"It can be about whatever the fuck you want. Okay, you're stuck on shit with the dog, so how about this: Can dogs recognize shapes? How does that sound?"

It sounded good. I loved Brownie, so I was glad he could be part of my experiment. My dad helped me outline exactly how the experiment would work. Basically, every day I would hold up in front of the dog three pieces of paper, each of which had a drawing of either a triangle, circle, or square. I would give him a treat every time I held up a circle, tell him to sit every time I held up a square, and do absolutely nothing every time I held up the triangle. After fifteen days of training, I'd perform two days of trials when I'd hold up the drawings of the shapes without giving any of the corresponding rewards. The goal was to see whether or not he'd respond to the shapes in anticipation of the actions that had followed during the lead-up to the trials. I was supposed to record my findings in a journal throughout the entire seventeen days.

When I did my "research" the first day, it was really boring. The dog didn't understand what was going on; he just stared at me while I held up the pieces of paper, and occasionally licked himself. He mostly just wanted to play, so I started running around the backyard, having him chase me, until I got tired. My dad worked late every night, so he didn't know I wasn't following through with my experiment. He'd check in from time to time, and I'd tell him my research was going fine. I just assumed I had plenty of time. As long as I started seventeen days before we had to turn in our findings at school, I'd be fine. But then I forgot about the experiment altogether.

One afternoon, the teacher reminded us our experiments were due in three days, and my stomach dropped. My mom picked me up from school that day, and when we got home I ran into my bedroom and shut the door. I took out my journal and began making up fake results from my nonexistent tests, complete with fake corresponding dates. I figured that a sly way of hiding my laziness was to report that the dog had slowly started to recognize the shapes toward the end of the experiment. Then when I did the trials without the rewards, he'd reacted in such a way that I knew he recognized the shapes. I remembered hearing a story about Pavlov's dogs. Pavlov sounded like a madcap scientist, and this experiment sounded like one he might even have performed himself. This was enough reasoning for me.

My dad happened to get home early that day, and I heard him barrel through the front door right as I finished writing up the last of my "findings." I threw my pen across the room to get rid of any evidence of my fraud. Almost as if he knew what I was up to, my dad immediately came into my room.

"How goes the science life?" he asked on cue.

Before I could answer, he saw my journal and picked it up.

"All the data is in there, Dad."

He was no longer paying attention to me, just perusing the data. After turning the pages and digesting my results for a minute, he set my journal down on my desk and looked at me.

"So the dog recognizes shapes, huh?"

"Yeah, it's weird," I said, trying to sound ambiguous.

"Yeah, that is weird," he said. "You obviously don't mind then if I run a little test on the dog, just so I can see for myself," he added.

At that moment I went a bit numb. All I could think was that maybe somehow, some way, the dog would know the shapes and react how I had written down that he reacted. My dad grabbed the crumpled pictures of the shapes from the floor of my room and walked outside.

"Sometimes the dog doesn't do it, though. It depends on how he's feeling and stuff," I said, trying to cover myself for any possible outcome.

My dad wasn't listening. He called the dog's name, and Brownie ran over toward us. My dad proceeded to hold the first shape, a triangle, in front of Brownie's slobbering face. According to my "data," Brownie was supposed to do nothing when he saw the triangle. Which he did. Unfortunately that was also his reaction to the circle and the square, which he was supposed to react to by sniffing my hand, in anticipation of a treat, and sitting down, respectively. Brownie ran off, and my dad turned to me. He looked me in the eye with an eerie sense of calm.

"I'm going to give you a chance right now to tell me anything you want to tell me," he said.

I started crying immediately and, between heaving sobs and snorts, confessed that I had forgotten to do the experiment and faked the data. My dad grabbed my notebook, tore it in half, and attempted to hurl it over the fence. But the loose pages fluttered about like a disappointing confetti celebration. He started kicking them around and then, still not satisfied, grabbed one of the dog's toys and hurled it across the yard like a shot-putter going for the gold. When Brownie retrieved the toy and pranced up for round two of what he thought was their game of fetch, my dad exploded.

"ALL BULLSHIT! YOU WROTE ALL BULLSHIT!" he screamed.

"I thought you said you'd give me a chance to tell you!" I yelled back.

"Yeah, you told me, and then it was all bullshit, goddamn it!"

My mom hurried out to see what was happening. She calmed my dad down and led him up to their bedroom so they could talk. After about ten minutes, he returned to the backyard, still simmering.

"You have shamed the entire scientific community. Fucking Einstein, everybody."

I told him I knew that, and I was sorry.

"This is what I do for a living, goddamn it, and I take it very, VERY fucking seriously."

"I know you do."

"No. You don't know shit. So here's what's gonna happen."

He proceeded to tell me that I had to go to my teacher and confess that I didn't do my experiment and faked the data instead, and ask her if I could deliver an apology for cheating to my classmates.

"And if she says you don't need to do that, tell her tough shit, you're doing it anyway. And I want to see the statement you're going to read BEFORE you read it. I got final say."

The next day before science class I explained to my teacher what had happened, and when the bell rang she turned to my sixth-grade class and told them I had something to say. I got up and read my prepared statement, which opened with something like this: "To my classmates and to the science community, I have committed an act of fraud. I falsified my data, and in doing so, have taken a process that is important to the development of the human race and disgraced it." After that it went on for a few more lines, but no one, including myself, had any idea what in the hell I was talking about. In between sentences, I glanced out at thirty sixth-graders staring blankly at me. After I was done reading my statement, I sat down. The teacher thanked me, said a few words about cheating, and then we moved on.

When I got home that night, my dad asked me how it went. I told him I had read the apology and that the teacher had thanked me.

"I'm sorry I had to be so hard on you, but I don't want people thinking you're a lying sack of shit. You ain't. You're a quality human being. Now go to your room, you're grounded."

On Respecting Privacy

"Get the fuck outta here, I'm doing stuff."

On Showing Fear

"When it's asshole-tightening time, that's when you see what people are made of. Or at least what their asshole is made of."

On Hypothetical Questions

"No. There's no scenario where I'd eat a human being, so you can stop making them up and asking me, understood? Jesus, is this how you spend your day, just coming up with this shit?"

On Friendliness

"Listen, I know you hate playing with that chubby kid because his mom's a loudmouth, but it's not that kid's fault his mom's a bitch. Try to be nice to him."

On Fair Play

"Cheating's not easy. You probably think it is, but it ain't. I bet you'd suck more at cheating than whatever it was you were trying to do legitimately."

On Leaving My Toys Around the House

"Goddamn it, I just sat on your goddamned truck guy. . . . Optimus Prime? I don't give a shit what it's called, keep it away from where I like to put my ass."

On Child Safety

"Don't touch that knife. YOU never need to be holding a knife. . . . I don't give a shit, learn how to butter stuff with a spoon."

On Slumber Parties

"There's chips in the cabinet and ice cream in the freezer. Stay away from knives and fire. Okay, I've done my part. I'm going to bed."

On Sharing

"I'm sorry, but if your brother doesn't want you to play with his shit, then you can't play with it. It's his shit. If he wants to be an asshole and not share, then that's his right. You always have the right to be an asshole—you just shouldn't use that right very often."

It's Important to Know the Value of a Dollar

"Let's just shut the fuck up and eat."

Both of my parents grew up poor—my mom, in an underprivileged Italian community on the outskirts of Los Angeles (her mother and father both passed away before she turned fifteen, at which point she and her five siblings were split up between a few different relatives); and my dad, on a farm in Kentucky, where he and his family worked as sharecroppers until he was fourteen and his dad bought the farm.

"When I had an earache, my mom would piss in my ear to kill the pain," my dad once told me in an effort to illustrate the depths of his family's poverty.

"That just seems weird, Dad. Not something poor people do."

"Yeah, maybe that was a bad example," he said after thinking about it for a moment.

Regardless, my parents never missed an opportunity to remind me and my brothers that we had it good. "You prance around on your fucking skateboards and bikes like you're the goddamned Queen of

England," he used to tell us when we spent our weekends goofing off with friends and neglecting our chores.

Sometimes my parents worried that my brothers and I had it too easy; that we'd grow up not understanding the value of a dollar, or how it feels to struggle. Even before my mom attended law school and began working in poverty law, she spent a lot of her free time volunteering in the poor communities of San Diego. She worked with parents on welfare and with homeless families, organizing after-school programs or helping them become self-sufficient to get off welfare. Anytime I complained about anything, she'd invoke those families.

"Why aren't you eating your pasta?" she asked me one night over dinner when I was ten years old.

"It's got peas in it," I replied.

"So pick out the peas."

"Well, you know I don't like peas, but you put peas in it anyway. Why do you do that?" I whined.

"Excuse me? You're treading on thin fucking ice, buddy," my dad barked, looking up from his plate. "That's your mother. You and she are not equals. Here's her," he said, putting his hand high up above his head, "and here's you," he added, putting his other hand well below the table. "If she wants to serve only peas for the rest of fucking eternity you will sit there every goddamned day and eat them and say 'thank you' and ask for more."

"Why would I ask for more if I hate them?" I said.

My dad told me to leave the table and go to my room—or at least that's what I think he said, because he was screaming with a mouth full of peas. About a week later, my mom came home from her law school library a little later than usual to find my brother Evan and me sitting on the couch watching TV a few feet from our dad, who was leaning back in his recliner, half-asleep. She turned off the TV, rousing my dad, and told the three of us that she had an announcement.

"We're going to eat what impoverished families eat," she proclaimed.

"What does 'impoverished' mean?" I whispered to Evan.

"It means poor people or something," he said, worry lines spreading over his face like a spiderweb.

Our mom went on to explain that she had visited the grocery store where some of the poor families she knew through her volunteering shopped with their food stamps. She described the food, how only some of it was expired though all of it looked disgusting, and then capped off her anecdote with, "We're going to eat for a week only the food I purchase from that store, with the same budget as they do."

"Dad?" I said, turning to him in desperation.

"Dad thinks this is a great idea," my mom replied, before he could answer.

A couple days later our fridge and cupboards were stocked with the strangest-looking foods I'd ever seen. I remember thinking to myself, *Poor people eat a lot of stuff in cans.* Many of the cans' labels listed some kind of meat, and underneath the name of the meat, "in water." Ham in water, chicken in water, cubed beef in water. The bread came in a white plastic bag on which there were only four words: WHITE BREAD FRESH BAKED.

"How is this fresh baked?" I asked Evan, holding a limp, floury slice in my hand.

"I don't know. I guess at one point, someone baked it, and then it was fresh."

At lunchtime on the first day of our new food regime, I opened up the brown paper bag my mom had packed for me. The first item I pulled out was a foul combination of foodstuffs posing as a turkey sandwich. I held it up in front of me. The bread looked like two pieces of soggy sandpaper, and the turkey looked like it was made out of whatever Larry King is made out of: some kind of pasty white, stringy flesh.

"That looks fucking nasty," my friend Aaron said, staring at my sandwich like it was a mangled creature that had washed ashore after a tsunami.

That afternoon I came home and marched right into Evan's room. I asked him if his lunch bag was filled with the same inedible stuff as mine. It was. We each had thrown out our sandwich and the strange, carrotlike vegetables that came with it, and eaten only the block of white American cheese that completed the so-called meal. I wanted to revolt, but Evan has never been the revolutionary type, and I wasn't prepared to stage a unilateral rebellion. The only hope I had was that my dad was feeling similarly disgusted and would put an end to this madness.

A few hours later, while we boys were hanging out in the living room before dinner, my mom presented us with that evening's menu. "Turkey soup," she announced, wearing an apron and holding a large spoon, as strange smells emanated from the kitchen behind her.

I looked at my dad, who kept his eyes on the evening news, unfazed. I was nervous about my physical ability to consume the meal my mom was about to serve, and as I usually do when I'm nervous, I voiced a positive thought in an effort to will the best possible outcome.

"I like turkey, right?" I said.

My dad continued to stare at the television. "Are you asking me, or are you telling me?" he said without so much as glancing my way.

"I'm telling you, I like turkey."

"Okay," he said, pausing for a moment before adding, "What the fuck does that mean for me?"

I could tell he was in a bad mood, so I ended the conversation. Voicing my affinity for turkey had helped, and I felt more confident about being able to eat the soup.

A few minutes later, we sat down to dinner and my mom filled all of our bowls with a brown, chunky liquid that resembled what I imagine a grizzly bear's diarrhea looks like. There were white chunks in it as well as red chunks, and it was the consistency of a watery bowl of oatmeal. All of us looked at one another, even my mom. I stuck my spoon in the bowl and was careful to maneuver around the chunks and ladle up only liquid. I brought it to my lips slowly and purposefully, as if I were a spy ingesting a suicide pellet. Then I took a sip. And spit it out.

"Jesus H. Christ, we're trying to have a meal here, goddamn it," my dad shouted, dropping his spoon on the table.

"I can't eat this! I tried!" I said, as Evan laughed.

"You didn't try," my mom replied.

"I did! I can't eat it! It's too gross!"

"This is how poor kids eat. This is the point of us eating like this, to understand what people less fortunate than us go through," my mom responded.

"I understand! I just want to eat something else now!" I said as my eyes welled with tears.

"Everybody just be quiet. Let's just shut the fuck up and eat," my dad said.

Then he put a spoonful of soup in his mouth.

"Jesus Christ. This is god-awful. I can't eat this," he said after swallowing it.

"See!" I exclaimed.

"No, you two are eating this," he said, looking at me and Evan. "I'm not."

"WHAT?!?!" I shouted.

I got up, stormed out of the dining room, ran into my room, and slammed the door. I assumed that within in a few seconds, my mom would open the door, say something that would make me feel better, and invite me back to the table for a proper dinner, like spaghetti with meatballs or chicken and potatoes. In the meantime, maybe she'd even drive to Jack in the Box and buy me a spicy crispy chicken sandwich, my favorite, to make up for this unjust and traumatic culinary experiment.

Ten minutes went by, and no one knocked on my door. I made a pact with myself to not leave my room until someone came for me. Another ten minutes went by, then an hour, then three hours, and suddenly it was ten o'clock, my bedtime. I turned the light out and crawled into bed, fuming and hungry. Then suddenly my door opened.

"Hey, Mom," I said, trying to sound angry and assuming it was her tucking me in as she did every night.

"Nah, it's me," said my dad, his large, shadowy figure approaching me, lit only by the light from the hallway behind him.

"Oh. Hi," I replied coldly.

He sat down on the bed and laid his hand on my shoulder.

"You're a pain in the ass, but I love you," he said, then laughed to himself.

I didn't respond.

"I know you're pissed off. I even understand *why* you're pissed off."

"No, you don't," I said confidently.

"Oh please, you're ten. I think I understand a goddamned ten-year-old."

Our conversation was not making me less upset, and he could tell. The tone of his voice softened.

"I know you think if you're eating that shit, I should have to eat it. And then I said I wasn't going to and you had to, and now you're pissed off, yeah?"

"Yeah."

"I've been poor. So has your mom. There are a lot of things in my life that I try really hard to make sure you never have to experience."

"So why can't this be one of them?" I asked.

"Son, you're spending a week eating shitty food. Your mom spent her whole childhood hungry. When you get up and throw a fit like you did tonight, it makes her feel like shit. It's like you're saying you don't care what she went through. That make sense?"

I told him that it did, and he told me why my behavior had also upset him.

"Food was a huge part of my life growing up. It's how we made our living, not just what we ate. So when you throw a fucking tantrum about it, it gets to me," he said.

"But why do you not have to eat it? Mom's eating it, and she already knows what it's like. Why don't you have to eat it?" I persisted.

He sat quiet for a second, then took his hand off my shoulder.

"Well, two reasons. The first one is that I know the value of a dollar, because I work every goddamned day to make them—something you've never done."

"But Mom works, too," I interrupted.

"Well, that brings me to my second reason: Your mom's a lot fucking nicer than I am."

Then he kissed me on my forehead and left the room.

On Videotaping Christmas Morning

"Okay, smile when you open your present. . . . No, smile and look at the camera, dum-dum."

On Going Camping with the Family

"No, I'm gonna stay home. You can take a family vacation, and I'll take a vacation from the family. Trust me, it'll make both of our time more enjoyable."

On Receiving Straight As on My Report Card

"Hot damn! You're a smart kid—I don't care what people say about you! . . . I'm kidding, nobody says you're not smart. They say other stuff, but not that."

On Getting Stung by a Bee

"Okay, okay, calm down. Does your throat feel like it's closing up? . . . Do you have to take a crap? . . . No, that don't have anything to do with bee stings, it's just you're pacing back and forth, I thought maybe you had to go."

On How to Tell When Food's Gone Bad

"How the fuck should I know if it's still good? Eat it. You get sick, it wasn't good. You people, you think I got microscopic fucking eyes."

On Dealing with Bullies

"You're going to run into jerk-offs, but remember: It's not the size of the asshole you worry about, it's how much shit comes out of it."

On Silence

"I just want silence. . . . Jesus, it doesn't mean I don't like you. It just means right now, I like silence more."

Not Everyone's Balls Should Be Busted

"Shit, I forgot to pick you up, didn't I? . . . Sorry about that. Any-way, I'm not coaching that fucking team anymore."

When I was ten years old, my father, against his better judgment, volunteered to coach my Little League team. Six months later, in the spring of 1991, Sam Halpern's coaching career came to an abrupt and angry end.

When my dad moved to Point Loma, our seaside San Diego suburb, in 1972, it was mostly a military community. He had served in the navy, and the familiar atmosphere and like-minded residents made him feel welcome. Over the years, Point Loma's proximity to the beach made it a desirable neighborhood to the wealthy, and huge houses sprouted up all around our modest three-bedroom home. My dad was not pleased. "I refuse to become a fucking yuppie by proxy," he announced after a young couple moved in next door, replacing one of the last of the old military officers who had once lived on our street.

Consequently, when I was growing up, my local Little League

team, Tom Ham's Lighthouse, was filled with the children of these people my dad disliked, and for the most part, they were spoiled, disrespectful kids. I knew almost right away it probably wasn't the best idea that my dad coach this team, but he loved baseball, and he loved me, and I think in his mind he figured that was enough.

My dad's only rule as a coach was that all the kids play the same amount of innings per game, no matter their skill level. "It's Little League. You're all terrible for the most part, and that's okay. The only way you're going to stink less is by playing," he told us at our first team meeting.

So every game, my teammates and I rotated on and off the field, each of us playing four of the six innings. Sometimes the rotations wouldn't work out perfectly, and if someone had to sit out three of the innings instead of two, that someone would be me. "You're actually good, and you know it. These other kids, it's fucking waterworks when I take them out of the game," my dad said to console me.

"So if I cried, I could play? That's not fair."

"No, if you cried, I'd still bench you, and then I'd bench you more for crying about not playing an inning in a goddamned Little League game. You're my son, and life's a bitch."

During his first couple months as head coach, my dad did not exactly become a fan favorite among my teammates and their parents, who found his even-playing-time rule incorrigible. At one point during a game, one of the kids' parents started mouthing off at him from the stands, furious that his kid wasn't playing more.

"We're losing because of you! Why would you bench the best player?! It's moronic!" my snot-nosed teammate's father yelled.

"Best player? I don't know what fucking game he's watching," my dad mumbled to himself.

The parent kept at it, clearly oblivious to my dad's growing anger and frustration. When the inning was finally over, Coach Halpern burst out of the dugout and stormed into the stands.

"Everyone plays the same amount of innings, that's my rule. This ain't the goddamned World Series, it's Little League. Our right-fielder picks his butt all game, and *he* gets that rule. Why don't you?"

My dad's flare-up quieted the parents for the time being, but behind the scenes, I would hear rumblings from my teammates.

At fielding practice a week or so later, a kid named Marcus tapped me on the shoulder. I turned around and he said, "My dad says your dad is an asshole."

I wasn't sure how to respond, so I just stood there for a few moments. Finally, I responded, "No, he's not. Your dad's wrong."

Then a baseball hit me on my shin, and I turned and realized it had been my turn in the ground ball line, and my dad had just hit one at me because I wasn't paying attention.

"Pay attention, son! Don't stand there with your thumb up your ass."

My dad was not helping my case for him.

Each practice, the parents and the spoiled kids would get to him a little more. He wanted this experience to just be about teaching baseball, but it wasn't. It was more of an unwelcome exercise in tolerance and self-restraint.

Finally, the friction came to a head during a practice in May. The temperature was hot that day, and the kids decided they didn't feel like doing my dad's conditioning drills, which he had learned during his time in the navy. After a series of foul-pole-to-foul-pole sprints, one of them staged a revolt and refused to follow his orders.

"This is dumb. Baseball isn't about running. Any real coach would know that," my teammate shouted, standing defiantly in front of my dad.

The instant the sound of that kid's insubordinate voice hit our fearless leader's ears, my dad had the same reaction Bruce Willis has at the end of *The Sixth Sense* when he realizes he's been dead the whole time: complete shock and confusion, followed by deep breaths in an attempt to calm himself. My dad's efforts to remain cool were futile.

The argument spiraled out of control, ending with him screaming, "Coach your own goddamned team, then, and kiss my ass," to a group of fourteen kids and one terrified assistant coach named Randy, who was only coaching the team because his wife had left him and he wanted something to take his mind off of his misery. Randy wasn't the most emotionally stable human being at the moment.

"It's all yours, Randy! Have a blast!"

My dad stormed off to his car and took off. Unfortunately, in his anger, he had forgotten that he was my ride. We were three miles away from home, and at that moment, I wasn't about to ask anyone else's parents for a ride—the kids were all staring at me, and Randy looked like he was about to start crying—so I decided I'd just walk home.

An hour later, when I was about two blocks away from my house, my dad drove up alongside me and rolled down his window. "Shit. I forgot to pick you up, didn't I?" I nodded yes. "Sorry about that. Also, I'm not coaching that fucking team anymore."

After he removed himself from the head coach position, my dad still came to all of my games and followed the team closely. He and I would have our own practices on days when the team didn't practice.

"Randy doesn't know shit about the game. He throws a baseball like he's a woman playing darts."

So two days a week, we'd practice pitching, just him and me. Then one day as we were driving to the field for one of our practices, he took a different route.

"Where are we going? The field's the other way," I said.

"We're picking up Roger. He's gonna play with us," he said.

Roger was the weirdest kid on the team by far. He smelled horrible, like rotten fruit mixed with Old Spice. He was actually a pretty good pitcher, but he'd have mental breakdowns in the middle of innings and completely implode.

"Why are we picking up Roger?" I asked.

"I'm teaching you pitching. He's the other pitcher on the team. Figured I'd teach you both at the same time," he said.

We stopped in front of an apartment where Roger was waiting. And for the next couple weeks, Roger came and practiced with us. Afterward my dad would buy us both ice cream. I told no one, because I already wasn't the most popular kid on the team, and the last thing I needed was to be associated with Roger.

At our second-to-last game of the season, my team played one of our better opponents. I had pitched the first three innings and kept the game close. Then Roger came in and pitched the fourth and fifth and shut them down, as we took the lead in the bottom of the fifth. In the sixth, as Roger walked out to the mound, one of the parents from the other team got up from his seat in the bleachers and stood behind the fence that was ten feet behind home plate. His name was Steve, and he was a burly guy with a large beer belly. He looked like someone Popeye would fight while on shore leave.

Every time Roger started to throw, Steve would try to rattle him. "He can't throw strikes, just take the pitches! He's going to walk all of you," Steve yelled to his son and his teammates.

Steve shouted undercutting comments like that every single pitch to psych Roger out. And Roger kept throwing balls, each one worse than the last. Eventually, he was crying on the mound, throwing balls that were six or more feet out of the strike zone. Randy walked out to the mound and took Roger out, and when Roger sat down on the bench next to me in the dugout, he was sobbing. Randy put his kid in, and Randy's son, also named Randy, threw just like his dad and gave up about six runs. We lost handily.

After the game, my dad approached me and said, "Wait here with Roger. We're giving him a ride home. But I need to take care of something first."

He walked over to the parking lot, where Steve was helping his son pack up his stuff. I waited about thirty seconds, then followed, even though he told me to stay, mostly because I didn't want to hang out with Randy and Randy. They both always hugged everyone good-bye, instead of waving or giving high fives, and it crept me out.

As I approached them, I saw my dad and Steve talking heatedly. "It's part of the game, Sam," Steve said.

"Bullshit," my dad replied.

"Watch yourself, Sam."

"The kid's dad's a drunk. His family's a goddamned mess, and you know that. And you're sitting out there screaming at him, trying to rattle him like this is the goddamned Major League so your kid can win a Little League game? You're a grown man, goddamn it. What in the hell is wrong with you?"

At that point, Steve mumbled a few more things, then got into his truck with his son, Kevin, and drove off.

My dad took me and Roger for ice cream before dropping Roger off. We didn't say much on the ride home. I wasn't exactly sure what had gone on, but I knew that my dad was angry at Steve, and I figured maybe I could make him feel better somehow.

"I don't like Steve either, Dad. He's fat, and so is Kevin, and they think they're good at stuff, but they're only good cause they're fat and bigger than everyone else," I huffed.

My dad was silent as he parked the car in our driveway. Then he turned to me. "Son, I didn't understand one goddamned thing you just said. Take your cleats off before you get inside the house, I think you stepped in dog shit."

On My Eighth-Grade Graduation Ceremony

"They're celebrating you graduating from eighth grade? We just went to your sixth-grade graduation two goddamned years ago! Jesus Christ, why don't they just throw a fucking party every time you properly wipe your ass?"

On Puberty

"How's puberty treating you? . . . How do I know you're going through it? Oh I don't know, maybe it's the three hundred dick hairs you suddenly leave all over the toilet seat that clued me in."

On Asking to Have the Candy Passed to Me During *Schindler's List*

"What do you want—the candy? They're throwing people in the fucking gas chamber, and you want a Skittles?"

On Accidentally Eating Dog Treats

"Snausages? I've been eating dog treats? Why the fuck would you put them on the counter where the rest of the food is? Fuck it, they're delicious. I will not be shamed by this."

On Trying Out for the High School Freshman Football Team

"I ain't letting you try out, you're too skinny. . . . No, I hate to break it to you, but you can't do whatever you want, and you most certainly are not a man."

On Bob Saget's Demeanor While Hosting
America's Funniest Home Videos

"Remember that face. That's the face of a man who hates himself."

On Being Intimidated

"Nobody is that important. They eat, shit, and screw, just like you. Well, maybe not just like you. You got those stomach problems."

On the Medicinal Effects of Bacon

"You worry too much. Eat some bacon. . . . What? No, I got no idea if it'll make you feel better, I just made too much bacon."

Try Your Best, and When That's Not Good Enough, Figure Something Out Quick

"Oh spare me, being stuck in your bedroom is not like prison. You don't have to worry about being gang-raped in your bedroom."

My dad has always valued education and hard work. "If you work hard and study hard, and you fuck up, that's okay. If you fuck up and you fuck up, then you're a fuckup," he's said to me on more than one occasion. But there are a lot of other factors besides effort that go into a successful and enjoyable school experience. Probably the most important one is how you fit in socially.

When I entered junior high, I was five feet tall, weighed eighty pounds, wore gigantic glasses, and—according to my grandpa—sounded like a tiny woman. I sort of knew where I stood, physically, when on a trip to Sea World, a caricature artist drew a picture of me and it didn't look all that exaggerated. I was basically a character a lazy screenwriter might come up with while half-assing a script: stereotypical nerd. My mom thought "awkward" just meant I was creative. So when I was heading into seventh grade, she talked my dad into sending me to a performing arts school where all the kids were just as awkward. But after seventh grade, my parents decided that the school was a waste.

"I didn't see them make you *create* or *perform* anything the whole year. Kinda defeats the fucking point of paying extra money for you to go to a place called the School for Creative and Performing Arts," my dad said when alerting me that I was going to go back to public school.

By the start of eighth grade I still hadn't hit my growth spurt, and I looked the same as I had a year prior. In fact, I think my voice might actually have been higher. I had a good idea how eighth grade was going to go about five minutes into my first day.

"Justin Halpern," I announced when my homeroom teacher asked for my name.

A big kid with a mustache named Andre leaned over to me. "Eh, puto," he whispered.

"Yeah?" I said, nervous.

"Why you sound like a fucking bitch?"

Fast-forward a year later to when I entered high school. I had grown several inches, I felt more confident, and I was being called "fag" around 85 percent less. I had a few friends, and everybody who had picked on me in eighth grade basically left me alone now.

My dad noticed when I came home from school looking and feeling upbeat and content after the first week was over. "There's a hop in your step now," he said. "You look like you just finished taking a shit all the time."

But with my newfound happiness and social life, I started to neglect my classes. And after the first progress report of ninth grade, I had a 2.33 GPA, which I knew wasn't good, but I didn't think was all *that* terrible. My dad thought otherwise.

"Not that bad? This ain't fucking MIT, this is ninth grade! Look at this shit!" he said, holding the progress report up. "You got a fucking C in ninth-grade journalism? How does that even happen? You work for the *New York* fucking *Times*? Couldn't break that big corruption story? Jesus Christ. Unbelievable."

After my parents discussed in private how to handle my falling grades, my dad sat me down and told me that for the next week I wasn't allowed to leave my room, except to go to school and to the bathroom. They'd serve me my meals in my room.

"WHAT?!" I shouted. "That's ridiculous! Lots of kids get worse grades than I do. And it's a progress report! It's not even on my permanent record!"

"Blah-blah-blah, I don't want to fucking hear it. You're too smart for grades like this. It means you were lazy and didn't do shit," my dad replied.

"This is unbelievable! You're putting me in prison! This is prison! For a 2.33 GPA!"

"Oh spare me, being stuck in your bedroom is not like prison. You don't have to worry about being gang-raped in your bedroom."

The subject that was dragging me down the most was math, but the next day at school I found out that I wasn't alone. Two-thirds of the class received an F, including me. My teacher was a real tough guy, and he often told us that he wasn't going to hold our hands. We either got it, or he'd flunk us out.

On the first night of my imprisonment, my dad came home from work, tossed on some sweatpants, and strolled into my room.

"Get out your math book. We're gonna cure this case of the stupids," he said as he sat down next to me on my bed, pointing at a stack of books underneath a pile of my dirty clothes. "Jesus, open a window, it smells like death shit in here," he added.

As we started to go through the book, he realized that not only did I not know how to do any of the problems, I didn't understand the basics I needed to even tackle them.

"They didn't teach you this shit?" he asked.

I told him they hadn't, and then I told him what the teacher had said about either getting it or flunking out.

"What? That's bullshit. What kind of asshole says something like that? Me and this teacher are having a chat. I'm coming to your goddamned school tomorrow."

The next day, I sat at my desk in homeroom, terrified that at any moment my dad would show up. You know that feeling you get when you're going up a huge climb on a roller coaster, waiting for that first big drop to come? Imagine that, but then imagine, too, that you have diarrhea. Which I happened to have that day due to a combination of *queso fundido* I had eaten the night before at a Mexican restaurant and the boxes of Nerds candy I'd been downing all morning. I spent periods one through three running between my classes and the bathroom, praying that my dad didn't burst into my classroom while I was on the toilet.

Then, during fourth period, I saw him out in the hallway being pointed to my English classroom by a janitor. He walked over and waited by the door, pacing back and forth, holding his briefcase. I slumped down in my chair. This stoner kid named Brandon leaned over to me, and pointed at my dad.

"I bet that dude's from the fucking FBI or some shit," he said.

"He's not," I muttered.

When the bell rang, I walked out into the hallway, where he said, "Grab your shit. Let's go see your teacher."

"Can't we just do this after school, Dad? Why do you have to do this during school?"

"Son, relax. I just want to chat with the man. I'm not gonna rip his head off and shit down his throat," he said. "Unless he provokes me."

We walked up toward the bungalow on the outskirts of campus where my math class met. Kids were already starting to file in, and my crusty teacher was sitting in the corner behind his desk. He looked like Dustin Hoffman, if Dustin Hoffman's skin was made of newspapers that had been left out in the sun. My dad barreled into the room and walked right up to him. I lingered in the hallway, trying not to be seen.

"You're the math teacher?" my dad barked.

My math teacher looked up, annoyed.

"I am. Can I help you?"

The ten or so students who were already seated took notice.

"That there, outside, is my kid. He's in your class," my dad said.

I ducked behind a tree.

"Justin, get in here. What are you doing, son?"

I came out from behind the tree and walked up the steps into the bungalow.

"Now, you're flunking him, and that's fine. If he deserves to flunk, then flunk his ass out. But when I went through the math with him, he didn't even know the basic concepts, and said you never taught them," my dad said.

"This is an advanced math class, and if the students can't follow along, they should transfer to a class that's more suited to their skill level. I've been teaching this class for twelve years the same way," my teacher responded.

"I don't give a good goddamn how long you've been teaching this class. He tells me all these kids are flunking out, and they all think they're losers," my dad said as he turned and pointed at all the students sitting in the class—who, for the most part, hadn't thought they were losers. "That's when I got a problem," he added.

At that point I think my teacher realized he wasn't dealing with a normal angry parent, but rather with someone who was making him look like an idiot in front of his students, so he took my dad outside. I traded places and moved inside. All of my classmates were staring at me, as the room was almost full now. I sat down in my seat, avoiding eye contact. Every ten or fifteen seconds we'd hear words and phrases coming from outside: my teacher yelling "I will not tolerate this!" followed by my dad responding, "NO—NO! You *will* tolerate it!"

"Damn. Your dad is making Mr. Jensen his bitch. Niiiiiice," the kid next to me said, smiling.

After a couple minutes, our teacher came in, his leathery face now a little more bronzed with fury. My dad walked into the classroom as well, right up to where I was seated at my desk.

"Don't worry about paying attention, you're transferring classes tomorrow," he said before exiting.

At dinner that night, my dad acted as if nothing had happened, but right before I went to bed, he called me over to the couch in the living room where he was sitting.

"Let's be honest. You're not Einstein, but don't let assholes like that teacher make you feel stupid. You're plenty smart, and good at other stuff. You know that, right?"

"Yeah."

"Don't just say *yeah* like a fucking mope. Let me hear you say it. Say you know you're good at stuff."

"I'm good at stuff."

"That's right. You're good at stuff. Fuck that math teacher," he said. "Oh, one last thing," he added. "Tomorrow see your counselor before you go to class. I think they're transferring you to one of those math classes where everybody uses their calculator for everything."

On Missing the No-Hitter I Threw in High School to Watch the Kentucky Derby

"A no-fucking-hitter?! And I missed it. Shit. Well, the Derby was fantastic, if that makes you feel any better."

On Missing My Second (and Only Other) No-Hitter a Year Later for the Exact Same Reason

"You have to be fucking kidding me! They need to stop scheduling these games on Derby Day. That's just silly."

On Friendship

"You got good friends. I like them. I don't think they would fuck your girlfriend, if you had one."

On Friendship, Part II

"I don't need more friends. You got friends and all they do is ask you to help them move. Fuck that. I'm old. I'm through moving shit."

On Accidentally Breaking Dishware

"Jesus, it's like going to a fucking Greek wedding with you. You need to master the coordination thing, because right now it's busting your balls."

On Going to a Party with No Adults Present

"Not a fucking chance. . . . Yeah, you're responsible, but I've seen those kids you go to school with, and if they weren't so stupid, they'd be criminals."

On Using Protection

"I'm gonna put a handful of condoms in the glove compartment of the car. . . . I don't give a shit if you don't want to talk about this with me, I don't want to talk about this with you, either. You think I want you screwing in my car? No. But I'd much less rather have to pay for some kid you make because there ain't condoms in there."

On Choosing One's Occupation

"You have to do something you love. . . . Bullshit, you clearly have *not* heard this speech before, because you're working at Mervyn's."

On Waiting in Line to See *Jurassic Park*

"There is no movie good enough for me to wait in a line longer than the run time of the movie. Either we're seeing something else or I'm leaving, and you can take a cab home."

At the End of the Day, You Have to Make the Best Decision for Yourself

"I'm not about to take the fall for somebody else's porn movie."

One day when I was fourteen, my friend Aaron barged through my front door after school, out of breath and sweaty. I could tell by the intense look on his face that whatever he was about to tell me just might be the most important thing I had heard in my entire life up to that point. It turned out I was right.

"Dude. I found a porno movie in the alley behind 7-Eleven," he said.

From his backpack he pulled out a VHS copy of *New Wave Hookers,* whose weathered, stained cardboard packaging left no question as to the fact that someone else had gotten his money out of this puppy. We reacted like a pair of farmers who had discovered a bag of money in one of their cornfields: jubilant, then immediately paranoid and distrustful of each other. But we knew we had to work together to make sure we didn't blow this opportunity and decided that the best idea was to take a time-share approach. I would take the porno the first and third weeks of every month, and Aaron would take it the second and fourth.

Though I watched the movie fifty-plus times, to this day I'm not sure what the plot line of the film is, because I never made it past the first twenty minutes. The only place I could watch it was in my parents' room. They had the only VCR in the house, which made me feel like a gazelle finding out that the only watering hole in a thousand-mile radius was inside a lion's den. Never once, though, did I think, *It's not worth it.* I'd wait until my parents had left the house, and then go into their room and do my business. I even worked out a plan for when I heard the front door open: I'd pull my underwear up from around my ankles as I hit EJECT, and then in one motion, remove the tape and hit the TV/VIDEO button so that they wouldn't know the VCR had been used. It was a well-thought-out, efficient plan, and it never failed.

Unfortunately I still got caught.

I woke up one morning to find my dad hovering above me, waving my copy of *New Wave Hookers* like it was a winning lottery ticket. I had violated the cardinal rule of watching porn: Don't leave the evidence in the VCR.

"I don't give a shit if you watch porn, watch away," he said. "But (a) don't do it in my room (the last thing I need is to come home from work and sit on some of your nasty business); and (b) I can't have your mother finding porn in my room and thinking that it's mine.

Then that becomes my problem, and I'm not about to take the fall for somebody else's porn movie."

"Are you gonna tell Mom?" I asked in a panic.

"Nah, I'll keep quiet about it as long as you don't do that shit on my bed," he said with a twinkle in his eye.

I reached my hand up assertively, assuming that now that we'd had our man-to-man he'd give me the movie back. "Ha, nice fucking try." He turned and left with it under his arm, laughing.

Having your father find your porno and laugh at you is an embarrassing moment in a teenager's life. I experienced a far more embarrassing one the next morning when I awoke to find my mother standing above me, holding my copy of *New Wave Hookers.* My dad had turned me in!

When my mom finished describing the ills of the porn industry and detailing the unrealistic nature of the sex depicted in its products, all the while screaming at me, I marched out into the living room like a man who had traveled a long distance to avenge a death.

"Hey!" I shouted at my dad, who was eating his daily bowl of Grape-Nuts.

He looked up at me, making a face that said, "Be careful in choosing your next words."

"You told Mom about my," and then I silently mouthed the word *porn.* "You said you wouldn't!" I added at full volume.

He put down his paper, looked at me, and replied in a measured voice, "Yeah, I thought about that. Too risky for me not to tell her. You shouldn't have left that porno in our VCR. Your penis betrayed you, son. Made you think stupid. It won't be the last time that happens."

On an Elderly Family Friend's Erectile Dysfunction

"I don't know why people keep coming to me when they can't get hard-ons. If I knew how to fix that I'd be driving a Ferrari two hundred miles an hour in the opposite direction of this house."

On My Frequent Absences at High School Dances

"You bitch about not going, so why don't you just go? . . . So then find a date. . . . So then meet more women. . . . Jesus Christ, son, I'm not continuing on with this line of questioning, it's depressing the shit out of me. Do what you want."

On Practicing

"Nobody likes practice, but what's worse: practicing, or sucking at something? . . . Oh, give me a fucking break, practicing is not worse than sucking."

On Getting Rescued by a Lifeguard at the Beach

"What were you doing that far out? You can't swim. . . . Son, you're a good athlete, but I've seen what you call swimming. It looks like a slow kid on his knees trying to smash ants."

On Breaking the Neighbor's Window for the Third Time in a Year

"What in the hell is the matter with you? This is the third time! You know, at this point I think it's the neighbor's fault. . . . No not really, it's your fucking fault, I'm just in denial right now that my DNA was somehow involved in something this stupid."

On the Varsity Baseball End-of-the-Year Fund-raiser

"Just tell me how much money I have to give you to never leave this couch."

On Video Game Systems

"You can't have one. . . . Fine, then go play it at your friend's house. While you're there, see if you can eat their food and use their shitter, too."

On the Importance of Watching the Evening News

"Let's finish talking in a bit, the news is on. . . . Well, if you have tuberculosis, it's not going to get any worse in the next thirty minutes."

On Appropriate Times to Give Gifts

"Yeah, I got him a gift. He got his kidney stone taken out. If you shoot a rock through your pecker, you deserve more than just a pat on the fucking back."

On My First Driving Lesson

"First things first: A car has five gears. What is that smell? . . . Okay, first thing before that first thing: Farting in a car that's not moving makes you an asshole."

Confidence Is the Way to a Woman's Heart, or at Least into Her Pants

"No one wants to lay the guy who wouldn't lay himself."

Between the end of my freshman year of high school and the beginning of my junior year, I grew ten inches. Suddenly I was six feet tall. "You're starting to look like a man, sort of," my dad told me on my sixteenth birthday, as I bit into a filet mignon he ordered for me at Ruth's Chris Steak House.

The downside of such a quick growth spurt was that I wasn't really in control of my body. I moved around like I was being puppeteered by someone with cerebral palsy. The good news was: Despite barely being able to walk ten feet without tripping over something, I could throw a baseball pretty hard. I was moved up to the varsity baseball team as a pitcher and led the team in wins and strikeouts.

That year, my school's cheerleading coach decided that in a show of school spirit, she was going to force her squad to attend all of the baseball games. Going to a high school baseball game is a lot like going to a student film festival; you're there because you feel obliged to someone involved in it, and after two repetitive, mind-numbing hours of "action," you congratulate that person and try to leave as quickly as possible. Needless to say, the cheerleaders mostly passed the time doing their homework and watching the grass grow on the sidelines. But my dad, who came to most of my games, thought otherwise.

"I've seen the way they look at you," he said as he drove me home after a game.

I tried to explain to him that they didn't look at me any way at all; that if they looked at anything during a game it was at their watches in hopes it was almost over.

"Bullshit," he said.

Fortunately, he left it at that. But not for long.

On Sundays, my dad would usually wake up early and head down to Winchell's Donut House, where he'd buy a dozen donuts for my family's breakfast, including six chocolate-glazed twists specifically for me. But on one Sunday in the spring of 1997, I woke up to discover there wasn't a box of donuts sitting on the dining room table next to the kitchen.

"Get dressed, let's go get some donuts," he said as I groggily padded into the dining room.

I tossed on a pair of basketball shorts and a T-shirt, and we headed out into my dad's silver Oldsmobile. When I tried to turn the car radio on and he quickly shut it off, I knew he wanted to talk to me about something.

Then we cruised right past Winchell's.

"I thought we were getting donuts," I said.

"Nah, we're going to have a real breakfast," he replied as he pulled into the parking lot at our local Denny's.

"This is Denny's," I said.

"Well, aren't you the fucking Queen of England."

We walked in, and my dad signaled to the hostess he'd like a table for two. A waitress led us to the far corner of the restaurant, where a small, square table was nestled right up against a larger rectangular table occupied by six hungover-looking college kids, including two guys who were wearing T-shirts commemorating a "solid rush class" for their San Diego State fraternity. The tables were basically attached, save for a leaf that had been folded under to provide some semblance of privacy. We sat down, and my dad told the waitress he wanted a couple glasses of orange juice for us. She left, and he turned his attention to me.

"I'm a man, I like having sex," he said.

The group of college kids next to us froze, then burst into muffled laughter. In a growing panic, I realized he was about to lay whatever his version of a sex talk was on me here, now, in Denny's.

"No—no, Dad. What are you talking about? Maybe we shouldn't eat here. I think we should go somewhere else. I don't think we should eat here. Let's go—let's go."

"What in the hell are you talking about? We just sat down here. Denny's ain't the best food, but you eat garbage like this shit all the time," he said right as the waitress dropped off two glasses of orange juice.

Out of the corner of my eye, I could see that the college kids were now focused on my dad and me like they had paid money to be there. I half-expected one of them to pull out a giant bucket of popcorn. Oblivious to my growing discomfort, my dad continued, telling me that in his day, he'd "had a lot of fun" and slept with, apparently, a significant number of women.

"I'm not that good-looking. Never was. But I didn't give a shit. You're not a bad-looking kid. Better-looking than I was. But nobody's paying either of us to take our picture, right?"

I nodded in agreement, and right as I did I heard one of the college kids say "wow," prompting his group of pals to burst into laughter again.

Then, my dad told me that the only way to meet women is to "act like you been there before. Don't worry about them telling you they don't like you. It's gonna happen. You can't give a fuck. Otherwise, guys like you and me will never get laid."

Our waitress was ten feet away and quickly approaching to take our order. I was crawling out of my skin. I felt like all of Denny's— all of San Diego—was listening, watching, and laughing, and I just wanted it to end. So I did something I rarely do to my dad: I cut him off.

"Dad, can you please get to the point you're trying to make? I don't want to talk about this the whole breakfast with all these people around us," I said, as I looked to my left and right, indicating that people were listening and that it was embarrassing for me.

He paused and looked around the restaurant, and then right at the college kids next to us, who quickly glanced away.

"You give a shit what all these people think, huh? Even though you never met a goddamned one of them," he said.

He nodded, grabbed the newspaper next to him, and began reading, which was almost more awkward, since now I had nothing to do but stare at the flip side of his paper, alone with my humiliation. We ordered our food and sat in silence until the waitress returned with my dad's scrambled eggs and my pancakes.

"Dad. What was the point you were trying to make?" I said, finally, in a hushed voice.

"Son, you're always telling me why women don't like you. No one wants to lay the guy who wouldn't lay himself."

"That's all you were gonna say?" I asked.

"No. But if you give a shit about what a bunch of people in Denny's think about you, then the rest of what I was gonna say doesn't even matter."

I told him to stop reading his newspaper, and he put it on the greasy table and looked me in the eye.

"So is that why you took me here? Some kind of test to see if I'd get embarrassed?"

"Son, do I look like the type with a master fucking plan? I just wanted to talk to you and eat some eggs. Let me finish doing one of them."

On Yard Work

"What are you doing with that rake? . . . No, that is not raking. . . . What? Different styles of raking? No, there's one style, and then there's bullshit. Guess which one you're doing."

On Being One with the Wilderness

"I'm not sure you can call that roughing it, son. . . . Well, for one, there was a fucking minivan parked forty feet from your sleeping bags."

On Getting Rejected by the First Girl I Asked to Prom

"Sorry to hear that. Hey, have you seen my fanny pack? . . . No, I care about what you said, I told you I was sorry to hear it. Jesus, I can't be sorry and wonder where my fanny pack is at the same fucking time?"

On My Attempts to Participate in Urban Culture

"What the fuck are you doing on the floor writhing around? . . . I'm not sure what break dancing is, but I sincerely hope it's not what you're doing."

On Selling His Beloved 1967 Two-Door Mercury Cougar

"This is what happens when you have a family. You sacrifice. [Pause] You sacrifice a lot. [Long pause] It's gonna be in your best interest to stay away from me for the next couple days."

On the SATs

"Remember, it's just a test. If you fuck up, it doesn't mean you're a fuckup. That said, try not to fuck this up. It's pretty important."

On Picking the Right College

"Don't pick some place just because you think it'll be easy to get laid there. . . . No, no, that's a very good reason to pick a lot of things, just not this."

On Proper Etiquette for Borrowing His Car

"You borrowed the car, and now it smells like shit. I don't care if you smell like shit, that's your business. But when you shit up my car, then that's my business. Take it somewhere and un-shit that smell."

On Curfew

"I don't give a shit what time you get home, just don't wake me up. That's your curfew: not waking me up."

On Using Hair Gel for the First Time

"It looks fine, you just smell weird. I can't put my finger on it. It's like rubbing alcohol and—I don't know—shit, I guess."

Always Put Your Best Foot Forward

"A three-year-old doesn't have a license to act like an asshole."

About once a year when I was growing up my family would head to Champaign, Illinois, where several generations of Halperns would congregate at my aunt Naomi's house. Unlike my dad, his relatives are the mellowest, warmest, most nurturing people I've ever meet. Whenever we'd visit them in the Midwest, I felt like I was in a Christmas special; everyone wore bright, multicolored sweaters, and any time I saw an adult relative for the first time, he or she would exclaim, "Look at you! You're all grown-up and so handsome!" before turning to my mom and dad and saying with a smile, "Isn't he handsome?" My dad always responded the same exact way, which was to say, "Yeah, I'm waiting for the modeling checks to come in so I can retire," and then laugh for an awkwardly long period of time, sometimes to the point of wheezing because he was out of breath, while the rest of us stood around in our Technicolor sweaters quietly waiting for his cackling to cease.

At our annual reunion in Illinois in November 1997, we had quite a few of my little cousins running around the house. They were all great kids, but one in particular I found to be especially entertaining: Joey, who was three years old at the time. The last time I had seen Joey was a few months prior, at a cousin's house in Seattle, on his birthday. He was so excited it was his birthday that he had spent the better part of an hour running around my cousin's house at full speed, coming to an abrupt stop every minute or so in front of a relative and screaming, "IT'S MY HAPPY BIRTHDAY, OH YEAH!" He was like a tiny David Lee Roth pumping up the crowd at a Van Halen concert right before he sang "Jump." Every time Joey stopped in front of me, before he could blurt out his line, I'd egg him on by asking, "Joey's happy birthday?!" Then his eyes would go wide, as if I'd just levitated in front of him, and he'd shriek, "JOEY'S HAPPY BIRTHDAY, OH YEAH!" We did this probably twenty-five times until my brother Dan came up to me and said, "Dude, fucking stop it."

Now, a few months later, at this family gathering, I was seeing Joey for the first time since his birthday. The instant he saw me, his face broke out in a huge grin, and he ran up to me and screamed, "JOEY'S HAPPY BIRTHDAY, OH YEAH!" I laughed and told him it was nice to see him, but he didn't acknowledge my greeting in the slightest. He just kept saying his catch phrase over and over. For the first ten minutes or so, my relatives thought it was cute and smiled at him or affectionately tousled his hair. My dad had been in the bathroom the whole time Joey had been carrying on like a parrot on speed, and when he walked out, he simply said, "Hey there, Joey."

"JOEY'S HAPPY BIRTHDAY, OH YEAH!" Joey screamed before running off.

My dad turned to me. "It's Joey's birthday?"

I explained the situation, and in the midst of my explaining, Joey interrupted.

"JOEY'S HAPPY BIRTHDAY!"

"He and I need to have a talk," my dad said matter-of-factly as Joey dashed into another room.

My dad talks to everyone, no matter his or her age, as he would to a forty-five-year-old physicist, so I had a pretty good idea how this was going to go.

"Just let him tire himself out, Dad."

"He doesn't want people thinking he's an idiot, right?" my dad replied.

"He doesn't even know other people think anything. He's three."

"A three-year-old doesn't have a license to act like an asshole."

On cue, Joey once again ran full speed into the room and screamed, "JOEY'S HAPPY BIRTH—"

"No," my dad said, cutting him off.

Joey paused for a moment. "Joey's happy birthday?" he said, totally devoid of conviction.

"No, Joey, it's not your happy birthday. You need to stop saying to people it's your birthday."

Joey looked confused and horrified, like a stripper bursting out of a cake only to realize she's been accidentally delivered to a baby shower.

My dad knelt down to Joey's level and added, "It is not. Your. Birthday."

The next sound I heard was a high-pitched squeal coming from

Joey's mouth. Then tears began streaming down his face and he ran away, arms at his sides, dangling like two limp strands of overcooked spaghetti.

Completely ignoring the disapproving glances from nearby family members, my dad got up from his crouch and turned to me. "Hey, it's a tough realization it ain't your birthday, but he's a better man for it," he said with satisfaction.

On My Bloody Nose

"What happened? Did somebody punch you in the face?! . . . The what? The
air is dry? Do me a favor and tell people you got punched in the face."

On the Democratic System

"We're having fish for dinner. . . . Fine, let's take a vote. Who wants fish for
dinner? . . .Yeah, democracy ain't so fun when it fucks you, huh?"

On Remaining a Gentleman No Matter the Situation

"I personally would never go to a prostitute, but if you've paid money for
some strange, that doesn't mean you can act like an idiot once you get it."

On Getting My Own Apartment Even Though I Attend
College 20 Minutes from Home

"You want your independence, huh? . . . Every time you tell me about your
independence, I just replace that word with the word *money*. Then it's easy
to say no."

On Finding Out I Tried Marijuana

"Pretty great, right? . . . Really? Well, we differ in opinion then. Don't tell your mom I said that, though. Tell her I yelled at you and called you a moron. Actually, don't tell her anything. See, now I'm paranoid, and I didn't even smoke any."

On Giving Up a 450-Foot Home Run in My First College Baseball Game

"Jesus. That wasn't even a home run, that was a fucking space experiment that should be written about in science journals or something."

On Attending the Student Film Festival Where My First Short Film Played

"I enjoyed it thoroughly. . . . I know which one was yours goddamn it, it was the one with the car. . . . Well shit, I thought that one was yours, so I left after. Don't bust my balls, that festival was like sitting through a three-hour prostate exam."

On My Responsibility to Do Chores

"You're a grown man in college, but you still live in my goddamned house. Huh. That sounds way shittier for you when I say it out loud."

On Getting a Job as a Cook at Hooters

"You, my good man, are not as dumb as I first fucking suspected."

On Meeting My First Girlfriend, Who Worked at Hooters

"I thought she'd have bigger breasts. I'm just being honest. That's not a bad thing or a good thing, that's just a thing I thought."

You Have to Believe You're Worth a Damn

"You are a man, she is a fucking woman! That is all that matters, goddamn it!"

I am not the first Halpern son to live at home in his late twenties. In fact, my two older brothers, Dan and Evan, did so as well. Evan is nine years older than me, and, along with Dan, is the product of my dad's first marriage. Evan is pretty much the nicest, most considerate human being you could ever meet. Plus, he just might be the only person to graduate from Humboldt State University, in Northern California, who has never smoked marijuana. After college, Evan wasn't sure what he wanted to do, and he spent the next few years working various jobs in various cities. But at twenty-eight, he found himself living at home with me, my dad, and my mom, who raised him since he was seven and who he considers his mother. It wasn't exactly a high point in Evan's life.

At the time, I was going to college at San Diego State, also living at home, and working at the Hooters in Pacific Beach, a nearby beach town. My best friend, Dan, and I had applied for jobs there a year earlier as a joke, and lo and behold, Hooters was looking for cooks and hired us. Contrary to what a teenaged guy might think, it quickly became the worst job I've ever had. As soon as you get over the fact that you work around a lot of boobs, you realize the job entails a bit of cooking, a ton of cleaning, and trying to meet the needs of insecure women yelling at you to make their fries faster. I spoke openly—and frequently—about my hatred for my job to everyone I knew, always comforting myself with, "But it could be worse. I could be the dishwasher at Hooters."

So when Evan asked me, "Hey, could you get me a job washing dishes at Hooters?" I knew he was in a bad place. Even though he'd heard me vent endlessly about working there, he still wanted the job. So I got it for him.

Five nights a week, he would come from his volunteer internship at a sleep therapy lab and go straight to Hooters, where he'd start washing dishes in slacks and a dress shirt. Then he'd head home to sleep, and do it all over again the next day.

My dad was concerned that Evan seemed lost and unhappy, and even more concerned that he wasn't meeting any women.

"He's a fine-looking young man. Your twenties is a time for screwing and so forth. He needs to meet some women," my dad told my mom after dinner one night while Evan was scraping buffalo sauce off of plates at Hooters.

In an effort to liven up Evan's romantic life, my dad decided to step in.

"I got a woman for you, big dude," my dad said to him one night after he came home from work. (My dad calls Evan "big dude" since he's the tallest in the family.)

"I'm pretty busy, Dad," my brother responded.

But my dad had already set up a blind date, and my brother, unlike myself, rarely puts up a fight.

"You're going to like her," my dad said, and Evan nodded warily.

I was shocked that Evan didn't ask our dad more about her, but that's not his style. Later, when I questioned his reticence, he explained, "I sort of do what Dad says. You get mouthy with him, and then he yells at you. I always figured if you could stay the kid he yelled at, I wouldn't be that kid."

So, the next Saturday night, Evan asked to get off early from his dishwashing shift at Hooters. I was working in the front of the kitchen and spotted him on his way out. He was covered in dishwater and looked like he had fallen on a grenade filled with hot sauce and blue cheese dip.

"Dude, you going on the date with Dad's lady?"

"Yeah," he replied, half asleep. "I smell, like, really gross. I should probably shower," he added. And off he went.

When I got off work a few hours later, I crawled out of my disgusting Hooters uniform and drove home shirtless, in an effort to prevent my car from smelling like chicken and hot garbage. I jumped in the shower and, when I came out, found my dad sitting in his recliner in the living room, asleep. Then I heard the front door open and saw Evan walk into the hallway and tiptoe toward his bedroom like a cat in a cartoon trying to sneak past a sleeping dog. Unaware that he was trying to go to bed without talking to anyone, I immediately jumped in.

"How was it, dude? Was she hot?" I shouted excitedly.

My dad snorted himself awake, and a look of fear shot over Evan's face.

"Big dude, how'd it go?" my dad asked, closing his robe back up.

"It was okay, but I'm tired," my brother said, trying to slip off to his room.

"Bullshit. Get back in here, let me know how it went."

Although Evan is quiet and demure most of the time, every once in a while he snaps. This was one of those times.

"She's a resident in neurosurgery who used to be Miss Oklahoma or something!" Evan screamed, his eyes suddenly venturing into angry crackhead territory.

"I know—good stuff, right?" my dad said, confused as to why Evan was upset.

"NO! I'm twenty-eight, and I live at home! I wash dishes at FUCKING Hooters!"

Evan rarely cursed, and never, ever, ever cursed at my dad. I don't know if my dad was angry or shocked, but he got stern real quick.

"What is your fucking point?" he said.

"My point is it was humiliating to sit there with some woman that's probably used to dating doctors and models and whatever the fuck else!"

Then came the line that sent my dad into a frenzy.

"She's out of my league! It was humiliating!"

My dad looked down at the floor and mumbled quietly to himself "out of your league?" over and over, like he was Indiana Jones trying to figure out if what a weird tribal person had told him right before he died was a clue. Then he exploded.

"This is complete fucking bullshit!" he screamed.

At that point I left the living room and tried to hide in the hallway so I could still listen.

"Out of your league?! What fucking league are you talking about?! You are a man, she is a fucking woman! That is all that matters, god-damn it!"

After that I couldn't make out the yelling, but a few minutes later Evan stormed past me. I peered into the living room and could see my dad felt bad about what had happened. Normally after arguments, he wore a red-faced look of conviction that you see on famous world leaders addressing a hostile United Nations. This time he just looked sad. I went to bed, not wanting to agitate him.

Nobody talked about what had happened those next few days. I figured the argument had passed. Then, my dad came home from work about a week later and told Evan and me to get in the car, that we were going to dinner at Black Angus, which, in my opinion, was the Kansas City Royals of steak houses. Yes, it technically qualifies as a franchise, but it's not worth getting excited about.

"Black Angus?" I replied, a little disappointed.

"Don't be an asshole," my dad said.

We drove to Black Angus, where we sat down in a dark booth with cracked leather seats, and my dad ordered three porterhouse steaks, his favorite cut. I had no idea what my brother was thinking, but I was wondering why in the hell we were at Black Angus, given that this was not a holiday and there was no apparent cause for celebration. Generally, steak is eaten by my family only on special occasions.

My dad exchanged a few pleasantries, asked us how we were doing, how our week was, and then, as the waitress set down our steaks in front of us, he said, "I want to tell you a story about the time I get mono from a stewardess."

He dove into a long, convoluted story about meeting some stewardess, how they "spent some time together," and what followed.

"I told everyone I got mono from this stewardess. You know why? Because I couldn't believe a woman that attractive would be with a guy like me, so much that I was bragging about getting goddamned mono. Then I went into the hospital with fucking Guillain-Barré syndrome, and it was a whole mess, and I almost died. Anyway, my point is: It took me a long, long time to realize that I was worth a damn to women. You don't have to brag about getting mono."

The three of us sat quietly for a moment before my dad called the waitress over to our table and said, "Let's see a dessert menu, I'm feeling frisky."

Evan and I glanced at each other, unsure if we were supposed to comment on our dad's anecdote.

"Gee, Dad, that's a great story," I said sarcastically, trying to stifle my laughter.

Evan started giggling, which sent me into a fit of laughter. My dad shook his head.

"Well, you both can go fuck yourselves," he said. "I'm trying to impart some fucking wisdom about women."

This only made the two of us laugh harder, to the point that Evan was almost unable to breathe and nearby patrons looked sympathetically at my dad, pitying the man who had to suffer two such inconsiderate sons. But he just started chuckling as well.

"As long as you two jerk-offs are happy, I guess that's all that matters," he said, as the waitress returned with the dessert menu.

On Taking My First Girlfriend to Las Vegas

"Vegas? I don't get it, neither of you are old enough to gamble. You're not old enough to drink. The only thing you're old enough to do is rent a hotel and—ah, I gotcha. That's smart."

On Realizing He Was Starting to Shrink Due to Old Age

"I'm five foot eleven! I used to be six feet, goddamn it. Boy, going bald and shitting infrequently ain't enough for God, huh? Gotta rub it in, I guess."

On the Death of Our First Dog

"He was a good dog. Your brother is pretty broken up about it, so go easy on him. He had a nice last moment with Brownie before the vet tossed him in the garbage."

On Getting Dumped by My First Girlfriend

"Listen, I understand you're upset. But you're both nineteen, you can't think you were only gonna screw each other forever. That's just silly talk."

On My Attempt to Hide a Hangover

"Coming down with something? Please. You reek of booze and bullshit. Don't lie to a Kentuckian about drinking or horses, son."

On Shopping for Presents for His Birthday

"If it's not bourbon or sweatpants, it's going in the garbage. . . . No, don't get creative. Now is not a creative time. Now is a bourbon and sweatpants time."

Focus on Living, Dying Is the Easy Part

"When I die, I die. I could give a shit, 'cause it ain't my problem. I'd just rather not shit my pants on the way there."

Although my mother came from a Catholic family, and my father, though not religious himself, developed a great understanding of Judaism and its customs, they decided to raise me and my brothers in a totally secular home. My dad is not a fan of organized religion. He's a scientist, and he believes in science, and that's that. "People can believe whatever the fuck they want. A turtle is God, whatever, I don't give a shit. I got my own beliefs," he told me when I first asked him about God over breakfast at age eleven.

In fact, the only time I ever experienced any sort of religious education was when my mother insisted I get in touch with my "Jewish roots" and sent me to a day camp in north San Diego County for kids who had one Jewish parent and one Catholic parent and wanted to learn more about Judaism. I lasted about three sessions before the rabbi complained to my parents that I just kept asking him to prove how he knew there was a God.

"Well, what'd you tell him?" my dad said to the rabbi.

"I discussed the idea of faith with him, and how God—"

"Listen, I think he just hates giving up his Sundays learning about it. No offense," my dad said, cutting the rabbi off.

I never went back.

But my brush with religion had done nothing to abate my fear of death. Like a lot of people, I have always been afraid of death and plagued by the question, *What am I doing here anyway?* And having been raised with zero religion or spirituality, I never received any answers—or anything to comfort me when my anxiety got the best of me. Every once in a while I'd hear that someone famous or a friend of the family had died, and I'd start thinking about death and how I had no idea what was going to happen to me, where I would go, if I'd even be cognizant of what was going on. As my thoughts spiraled, my heart rate would quicken, I'd lose color in my face, and then I would have to lie down.

During a baseball practice in college, I heard that a kid I had gone to high school with had died in a car crash. As was par for the course, I got so light-headed I had to lie down. When my teammates and coaches asked *why* I was lying down on the field, I went with the obligatory no-one-will-question-this-excuse excuse: "I think I have diarrhea."

I realized then that while my paralyzing fear of death probably wasn't going to kill me, it was something I should learn to deal with in an adult way sooner rather than later. I decided to talk to my dad about it since he was the most unflappable person on the subject of death I'd ever met.

"When I die, I die. I could give a shit, 'cause it ain't my problem. I'd just rather not shit my pants on the way there," is a line I'd heard out of his mouth more than a handful of times. I wanted that same attitude. Or, at least, I wanted to understand how he was able to be so cavalier about it.

So one morning during college, when he was eating Grape-Nuts at the kitchen table and reading the newspaper, I sat down next to him and poured myself a bowl. After listening to us both crunch our way through two suggested daily portions of natural whole-grain wheat and barley, I spoke up.

"Hey, Dad. I have a question."

He peered over the newspaper to look at me.

"What is it?" he asked.

I began a very roundabout way of getting to the point, philosophizing about religion and the possibilities of heaven and hell, until he cut me off.

"Is there a question somewhere on the fucking horizon?"

"What do you think happens after you're dead?"

He set his paper down and scooped a big bite of soggy Grape-Nuts into his mouth.

"Well. It's nothingness for eternity," he said casually, then picked up his paper and began reading again.

"What do you mean, 'nothingness'?" I asked, feeling my heart start to beat a little faster.

He put down the paper again.

"Nothingness, you know. Nothing. Like, you can't even describe it because it's not anything. I don't know, if it makes you feel better, just picture infinite darkness, no sound, no nothing. How's that?"

My heart rate rose further, and I started to feel light-headed. I couldn't comprehend how he could believe this and be okay with it. Plus, his concept of death only added to my fears the fact that it was infinite. I've always had an obsession with keeping track of time. One night in college when I smoked pot, my roommates came home to find me sitting by the microwave, setting fifteen seconds on the timer over and over again so I could keep count of how many minutes were passing. Now I was being told that not only was there no afterlife, but what we all had in store was nothingness, an infinite period of it.

"How do you know that? You don't know that, it's just your opinion," I said.

"Nope. Not my opinion. That's what happens. Fact," he replied, pulling the paper back up and starting to read. I could feel I was about to pass out, so I stumbled away from the table and walked toward my parents' room, where my mom was sitting on their bed. Immediately she could see there was something wrong.

"Justy, you look terrible! What's the matter?" she said, patting the space on the bed next to her, ushering me to sit down.

I told her what my dad had said, and she tried to calm me down by telling me that obviously he had no idea what happens after we die.

"He's never been dead, and that's the only way you can know, right?" she murmured soothingly.

"Yeah, I guess you're right," I replied, not fully convinced.

My dad entered the room at that moment, and my mom looked him sternly in the eye and said, "Sam, tell Justin that you have no idea what happens when you die. He knows it, but just admit it."

"I will not. I know exactly what happens, and that's what happens." And he left the room.

I slept very little that night. I kept trying to wrap my head around the idea of infinite nothingness. The last time I had had that much difficulty sleeping was when I was fifteen years old and stayed awake half the night overanalyzing *Back to the Future II* and brainstorming all the parallel Hill Valley neighborhoods that would result from Michael J. Fox's traveling back and altering time. That time, excitement mixed with confusion kept me up; this time, it was sheer terror.

After tossing and turning most of the night, I finally gave up on sleep and dragged myself out of bed at 5:30 A.M. I strolled out of my bedroom to find my dad back at the kitchen table, eating Grape-Nuts. He asked me to sit down, so I did.

"Do you know the great part about infinity?" he said.

"No."

"It's never over. You, your body, the energy inside it, it all goes somewhere, even after you die. You're never gone."

Clearly, my mom had had a word with him.

"So you're saying you think we live forever? Like, ghosts and all that stuff?" I implored.

"No. Jesus Christ. You need to take a fucking science course or something. What I'm trying to say is that what makes you up, it's always been around, and it always will be around. So really the only thing you should worry about is the part you're at right now. Where you got a body and a head and all that bullshit. Just worry about living, dying is the easy part."

Then he put down his spoon, looked at me, and stood up.

"Now, if you'll excuse me, I have to do one of the best things about being alive: take a shit."

On Telemarketer Phone Calls

"Hello? . . . Fuck you."

On My Interest in Smoking Cigars

"You're not a cigar guy. . . . Well, the first reason that jumps out at me is that you hold it like you're jerking off a mouse."

On Entertaining the Notion of Getting a Tattoo

"You can do what you want. But I can also do what I want. And what I'll be doing is telling everyone how fucking stupid your tattoo is."

On House-Sitting

"Call me if something's on fire, and don't screw in my bed."

On the Television Show *The X-Files*

"So, the woman and the dopey-looking guy screw, and then they look for aliens—or they just screw and sometimes aliens follow them?"

On Deciding to Use His Senior Discount for the First Time

"Fuck it, I'm old. Gimme free stuff."

On Whether to Vote for George W. Bush or Al Gore

"Gore seems kind of like a pompous prick, but every time I see Bush I feel like he's probably shit his pants in the last year, and it's something he worries about."

On My Trip to Europe

"I know you think you're going to get all kinds of laid. It's not a magic place, it's the same as here. Don't be stupid."

On Baseball Cards

"If you sell them over the age of twenty, it means you either never get laid or you have a drug problem."

Don't Be So Quick to Buy into What Authority Prescribes

"What I'm saying is: You might have taken care of your wolf problem, but everyone around town is going to think of you as the crazy son of a bitch who bought land mines to get rid of wolves."

At about nine years old, I started developing a strange, uneasy feeling in my joints. It felt kind of like a little tiny person was inside them, tickling me. I wasn't in pain, but I was uncomfortable a lot of the time, and the sensation had an unfortunate side effect: it caused frequent muscle spasms. My mom encouraged me to see a doctor, but the physician I went to couldn't find anything wrong with me. "He's growing fast, and it's taking a toll. It's natural. It will pass," he said.

My brother Dan offered a different diagnosis: "Maybe it's because you're a gay," he suggested one night, after I had complained to my dad for the umpteenth time at dinner.

"Quiet," my dad barked at my brother. "Does it hurt?" he asked me.

"No. It's just, I don't know. Weird."

"Thank you for that detailed description, Ernest fucking Hemingway. If you're not feeling pain, then what's the problem?"

"I don't know, it makes me have to stretch and stuff," I responded.

"He twitches all the time, Dad," my brother chirped.

"Your mouth twitches all the time," my dad snapped at him. Then he turned to me. "Okay, well, if it starts hurting, let me know."

From that point forward, everyone in my family referred to the uneasiness in my joints as The Twitches, which sounds like some kind of eighteenth-century sexually transmitted disease British aristocrats got from prostitutes, but it was a catchy name, and it ended up sticking.

When I was growing up, my dad personally selected my primary care doctor. For the most part, he picked doctors he had professional relationships with. The one time I expressed annoyance at having zero say in choosing my doctor, he snapped, "I'm sorry, did you go to medical school? Did you spend the last twenty-five fucking years of your life in medicine? No, you did jack shit. Let me handle picking your doc, and do me a favor and put a thumb in your ass and be quiet."

But when I was twenty-one years old, my physician moved away, and when my insurance company gave my dad a list of doctors to choose from, it turned out that he was unfamiliar with all of them. So he let me review the list and pick out a doctor myself.

"Okay, listen, this is going to sound biased, but pick someone with a Jewish last name," he instructed me.

"That's racist, Dad."

"Racist? Oh give me a fucking break. It's not racist, I just know a lot of Jewish doctors and they're good. And let me remind you that I'm a Jewish doctor and—you know what? Fuck you, pick whoever you want," he said as he stormed out of the living room.

So I picked a doctor at my dad's hospital, and a few months later I went in for a routine checkup. The doctor was a young guy, short, with dark hair. He was like a Jewish Tom Cruise . . . with a lisp. We went through all the normal checkup routines: breathe in and out, turn your head and cough, slam the minihammer on my knees, etc.

"Okay, you're healthy," he said, as we were wrapping up. "Is there anything else?"

I thought about it and was about to say no, but then remembered The Twitches and figured I might as well speak up. I described my symptoms, and he spent the next few minutes asking questions and doing a few more physical tests, moving my legs back and forth, pressing on my joints. He asked me to wait in his office and left the room for a couple minutes.

"Listen, there's a drug called Zoloft," he said as he entered his office with a prescription pad in hand. He launched into a description of Zoloft and its history, and told me that he thought it might help me.

"I don't know that it will, but it might. You might be able to get rid of your joint problems entirely. I think we should take a shot," he said.

I told him I'd love to, and he wrote me a prescription, which I took straight to the pharmacy and got filled.

That night, my dad and I sat down to dinner just the two of us, since my mom was working late. When he asked me how my doctor's appointment went, I told him that I was given a clean bill of health.

"Oh, also, he prescribed some stuff for The Twitches," I added.

"What kind of *stuff?*" he asked, his eyebrows furrowing into a steep mountain of hair.

"Well, you know, the doctor was talking about how he wasn't sure what was causing my twitches so, you know. . . ."

"No, I do not know. Enlighten me," he said between clenched teeth.

I told him I'd filled a prescription for a drug called Zoloft.

"Bring me those fucking pills right now!" he shouted, holding out his hand as if I were going to make them magically appear.

"What? Why? What is your problem?"

"You have no idea what that shit is for. It's an antidepressant. It's for depressed people. Are you depressed?"

I told him that I didn't think I was, but that I was tired of having The Twitches. They kept me up at night, and I always sounded ridiculous when I tried to explain to people why parts of my body would suddenly jerk.

My dad took a deep breath.

"You're making that face like you gotta shit. Calm down for a moment," he said. Then he sat back in his chair.

"Listen. Imagine you own a farm. On that farm, you got a bunch of sheep. And every night, wolves come and kill your sheep. It's a problem, you want to fix it. Now, you could go and put a bunch of land mines around your farm, and every time one of the wolves comes near your farm, it steps on one of them land mines and blows it to fucking pieces. You think, 'problem solved,' right?"

He stared at me for a few moments, until I realized he wanted me to answer that question.

"I have absolutely no idea what you're talking about right now," I said.

"Jesus Christ, you're fucking obtuse. What I'm saying is: You might have taken care of your wolf problem, but everyone around town is going to think of you as the crazy son of a bitch who bought land mines to get rid of wolves. That's how they'll treat you—in fact, that will be the first thing they associate you with. And not only that, now the only way you know how to get rid of wolves is blowing them the fuck up. You get what I'm saying now?"

He sat back in his chair, and a few moments of silence passed as the two of us stared at each other.

"Dad, I'm taking the pills."

"Goddamn it! The hell you are!"

He shot up out of his chair and stormed into my room. I heard him rooting around furiously, opening and closing drawers, unzipping and rummaging through my backpack. When he returned to the dining room, he was holding my bottle of Zoloft. He marched over to the sink, poured the $20 worth of pills down the drain, and turned on the garbage disposal for good measure.

"You'll thank me later," he said as he returned to the table and resumed eating.

"What in the hell do I tell the doctor?" I asked.

"I don't give a shit. Go back to your doctor and tell him to kiss my ass."

A few weeks later, my dad came home early from work and popped his head into my bedroom, where I was doing homework.

"Grab a snack to take with you. We're gonna go down to the hospital," he said.

"Why? Please don't harass my doctor."

"Give me a fucking break. I'm not a maniac."

I got in his car, and we drove to UCSD Medical Center. We walked into the waiting area, where my dad approached the reception desk and checked us in. Two minutes later, the nurse called my name and led my dad and me back to a room where an older, gray-haired doctor was waiting.

"Sam, good to see you," the older doc said, extending his hand to shake my dad's.

They chatted for a couple minutes, making incomprehensible doctor jokes that ended with punch lines like, "and then it turned out it wasn't even a goddamned myocardial infarction!" followed by hysterical laughter. I sat atop the doctor's table, stone-faced and trying to minimize the rustling noises emanating from the thin white paper that coated it, while I waited to be acknowledged.

"So, what can I do you for, Sam?" the doctor said.

"The kid's got some uneasiness in his joints. I was hoping you could help him, because it's really a pain in his ass. Tell him, son."

"Well, it sort of feels like I'm being tickled from the inside of me—"

"Goddamn it, use medical terms, he's a doctor," my dad barked.

The old doctor performed the same tests my other doctor had and then turned to my dad, as if I wasn't in the room.

"I think the culprit here is your boy had quite a growth spurt, and it put a lot of strain on his joints. Now he's feeling the effects of it."

"So you're saying he grew funny, huh?" my dad replied.

"Well, more or less, yes."

At last I had an answer.

We left the doctor's office and, as we were walking down the hospital hallway, my dad turned to me and whispered, "Shit. I could've told you that. Fucking doctors, huh?"

On the Proper Technique for Growing a Garden

"It's watering plants, Justin. You just take a goddamned hose and you put it over the plant. You don't even pay rent, just do it. Shit."

On Moving Out of My Parents' House for the First Time

"I'd say I was gonna miss you, but you're moving ten minutes away, so instead I'll just say don't come over and do your fucking laundry here."

On Furnishing One's Home

"Pick your furniture like you pick a wife; it should make you feel comfortable and look nice, but not so nice that if someone walks past it they want to steal it."

On Coming Over to My New Apartment Unannounced and Seeing My Room for the First Time

"Why is there a mural of two people fucking on your wall? . . . Son, let me be the first to tell you that you're not Andy fucking Kaufman. When you get famous maybe shit like this will be funny, but right now all it says to me is this kid never gets laid. Ever."

On My Response to Having My Tires Slashed

"Oh, don't go to the goddamned cops. They're busy with real shit. I don't want my tax dollars going to figuring out who thinks you're an asshole."

On Living on a Budget

"Why are you going over your monthly expenses? . . . No, let me shorten this process for you: You make dog shit, so don't spend any money."

On My Friend's Response to Getting a Minor-in-Possession Ticket

"He cried? Jesus, don't ever have that happen to you. . . . Well, no, try not to get a ticket, sure, but if you do, don't cry like a fucking baby."

On Getting an Internship at Quentin Tarantino's Production Company

"That is one ugly son of a bitch. . . . Oh, yeah, no, congratulations. If you see him, try not to stare at his face if you've eaten anything."

On My Interest in Going Skydiving

"You won't go do that, I know it. . . . Son, I used to wipe your ass, I know you better than you know you. . . . Fine, Mom used to wipe it, but I was usually nearby."

On the Arm Injury That Ended My Baseball Career

"I'm really sorry, son. If you're pissed off and you need to blow off some steam, let me know. We'll go smash some golf balls or something. . . . Oh right, the arm. Well, there's other, nonphysical ways to blow off steam."

On Pringles Flavors

"I'm not eating something called 'pizzalicious.' That's not even a fucking adjective. You can't just add 'licious' to nouns. That's bullshit."

You Never Stop Worrying About Your Children

"They'll gut you like a pig, piss on your corpse, and then say 'Welcome to Mexico!'"

By my junior year of college, I had moved out of my parents' house and into a three-bedroom house in Pacific Beach, San Diego, which I shared with my best friend, Dan, and a girl we were friends with. Even though my new place was only ten minutes away from my parents', it might as well have been in Sweden for all my dad cared. There was no way he was going to visit.

"I don't want to know what goes on in that house," he said when I finally asked him if he wanted to come check it out.

"Dad, there's nothing bad going on in the house."

"No. You're not understanding me. I don't *care* what goes on in that house. It's called *apathy*. Look it up."

I was living on my own, but I still headed home once a week to do my laundry, raid the fridge, and take advantage of anything else I possibly could while I was there.

"You just barge in and take whatever you want, whenever you want. It's like you're the goddamned SS and I'm living in fucking Nazi Germany," my dad said after coming in from the backyard, where he was watering his roses one afternoon, to find me in the kitchen eating the bagel with cream cheese he had prepared for himself just moments earlier.

Even though he wouldn't admit it, I always knew my dad was happy to see me when I came home. I'd usually head over at night, when he was home from work, and we'd have a nice chat about things that were going on in each other's lives. It was the first time I had ever felt like I had an adult relationship with my dad. We were growing closer and becoming friends. I realized that we'd really broken down some barriers one evening in late June when he asked me to help him with a project in his garden that Friday.

"Friday, come over at four. Don't be late, I don't want to be fucking with this after dark. I'll buy you dinner afterwards," he offered.

Since he'd purchased the house in 1972, my dad's garden had taken over almost every spare inch of our yards, front and back, and he'd planted not only flowers but tomatoes, lettuce, even corn. He loved his garden and spent most of his free time taking meticulous care of it. He was also very particular about who touched it. That Friday he was going to put up some fencing to grow tomatoes, a difficult job for one guy. He normally did the tough jobs on his own anyway. One time many years earlier I had tried to help him on a similar project and while bending the wire fence to wrap it into a cylinder, my hand had slipped and accidentally released the metal, which whipped around and stabbed my dad in the leg.

"GODDAMN IT FUCK!" he had screamed in pain, before turning to me and adding, "GO! AWAY!"

So when my dad asked me to help out on his garden that coming Friday, the request meant a lot to me. He didn't need my help—he *wanted* it.

On Thursday, the night before I was supposed to help him out, I was studying with a girl named Stacy from my communications class. We were taking a summer school course because each of us had dropped a class during the school year. I had been in a few classes with Stacy before and had developed a major crush on her. I had never asked her out or even hinted at my feelings, mostly because she had a boyfriend, but even if she hadn't, I doubt I would have gotten up the courage to make a move. She was blond, with large breasts, which I had pictured in my head numerous times during a variety of different fantasies I played out while masturbating. As we sat studying on a futon in her bedroom, she turned to me and said, "I've got to tell you something. Peter and I broke up."

This was exactly how 96 percent of all my masturbatory fantasies of her started.

"I can't study right now. I can't concentrate. I want to do something fun. You want to do something fun?" she asked.

"Yes," I said, trying to act cool.

"Some of my friends and I are going down to Rosarito tonight for the Fourth. We rented a hotel room. You should come."

She could have said, "Some of my friends are going to shove bottle rockets in our asses and then light them and shoot them at a police station—you should come," and I would have said yes.

I told her I needed fifteen minutes to pack my stuff and strutted as calmly as I could out of her house. Then I dashed through the dark to my car, where, with beads of sweat forming at my temples I pressed my foot all the way down on the accelerator. Unfortunately the top speed of my 1986 Oldsmobile Brougham was around fifty-seven miles an hour, so it took me longer than I hoped to get home. I nervously tossed a few shirts, a pair of swim trunks, and every single condom I could find—which was about thirty—in my backpack. I drove back to Stacy's house and she; her three best girlfriends, who had arrived in my absence; and I hopped in her friend's Chevy Blazer and took off for Mexico.

A small Mexican beach town right next to Tijuana, Rosarito is a lot like the bleachers in Fenway Park during a Yankees–Red Sox game: crowded, dirty, and filled with thousands of loud, drunk Americans who haphazardly throw their garbage on the ground. Yet somehow it's still kind of charming. Rosarito's biggest draws are that the drinking age is eighteen, and everything is dirt cheap. The five of us spent the ride down the Pacific Coast Highway drinking Tecates and talking excitedly about how drunk we were going to get as soon as we arrived in Mexico.

"I'm gonna get so fucking wasted," Stacy's friend in the passenger seat said. "Justin, are you going to get fucking wasted, or are you gonna be a fag?" she asked, turning to me.

I wasn't sure how she decided those were the only two paths to go down this weekend, but I clearly saw the direction she was hoping I would lean toward.

"I'm getting fucking wasted!" I screamed, trying to match her intensity.

Apparently I did, because everyone cheered, and then Stacy grabbed my crotch. It was a pretty unsexy move—and sort of hurt—but any interaction my crotch had with Stacy's hand was welcome.

A couple hours later, we pulled up to our hotel in Rosarito and checked into our dingy room, which contained only one bed, a bathroom, and three different paintings of a large-breasted Mexican woman being carried off by a Spanish conquistador. We immediately started taking shots of tequila from the bottle we had purchased at the hotel's gift shop. I went into the bathroom and put one condom in my sock and one in my baseball hat, just in case Stacy and I didn't make it back to the hotel room. I threw some water on my face, patted my hair into place, and brushed my teeth.

When I came out of the bathroom, all three of Stacy's friends were crowded around her, and she was curled up in a ball on the floor, crying hysterically.

"I miss Peter! I can't believe we're fucking broken up!" Stacy sobbed as her friends tried to calm her down.

Then Stacy got up, ran past me to the bathroom, and vomited in the toilet. For the next day and a half, Stacy sat in the hotel room with her friends, bawling and rehashing every detail of the breakup. A couple times I went out to a bar by myself, stood around for an hour, talked to no one, then went back to our room, which still reeked of vomit.

On Saturday afternoon, we piled into the Blazer and drove silently back up the coast to the U.S.–Mexico border. Stacy sat next to me the entire time, sleeping. As we crossed the border, I turned my cell phone back on, since I hadn't had reception in Mexico. It began buzzing to indicate that I had new messages. As I punched in my voice mail access code, it dawned on me that I had forgotten to help my dad with the garden.

"You have four new messages," the robotic voice declared. I was half expecting it to add, "You are so fucked."

The first message played. "Son, it's Dad, I need you to pick up something from the Home Depot before you come over. Call me back."

"Next message," the robotic voice mail alerted me as I began to feel nauseous.

"Son, where the fuck are you? I said to be over at four, right? It's four-ten. Call me."

The next message contained just a few moments of silence, and then the sound of hanging up. I felt a little relieved. Maybe he was over it by now.

"Next message, received today at three-thirty P.M.," said the robot.

"WHAT IN THE FUCK IS GOING ON? I stopped by your place and your roommate said you're in Mexico! Are you in fucking Mexico?! CALL ME!"

I started sweating and couldn't keep my legs still, which was unfortunate, seeing as we were just about to drive through the border patrol inspection. The officer waved us through even though I'm pretty sure I looked like I was sitting on about two thousand pounds of cocaine and hiding a half dozen illegal aliens in our trunk.

Once we were across the border, Stacy's friend pulled over at the first exit.

"I am totally fiending for some Jack in the Box," she said.

"No. I need to go home right now," I snapped, my voice ascending to a note I hope no woman ever hears out of my mouth again.

"Whoa, chill out. We're just gonna grab some Jumbo Jacks—God."

In my head, I was fantasizing about jumping into the front seat, drop-kicking her out of the car, slamming the door, and stepping on the gas. Instead I just sat in the dining area of the Jack in the Box while the four girls leisurely enjoyed their hamburgers. I called Dan to see how much damage was done.

"Your dad looked all pissed off. I told him you were in Mexico," Dan said.

"You told him I was in Mexico?! Why did you tell him I was in Mexico?!" I screamed.

"Because you were in Mexico."

I hung up the phone. Shortly after, Stacy and her friends moseyed back to the car. We continued our drive up the coast and, upon reaching San Diego, headed to Stacy's apartment, where my car was parked. I grabbed my travel bag out of the back of the Blazer and briskly walked toward my car.

"Um, okay—bye?" Stacy said snidely.

"Yeah, yeah, bye—sorry," I replied, jumping into my car and slamming the door.

I began the drive over to my parents' house, trying to figure out what lie I could tell to diffuse the situation. I came to the conclusion that there really was no diffusing this because it had too many volatile elements: I blew off my dad; I disappeared and was unreachable; and—the final straw—I had gone to Mexico. My parents had irrational fears of Mexico and assumed that once you crossed the border, drug runners made you swallow a heroin balloon and then within the hour you were in a bathtub full of ice and they were harvesting your kidneys.

As I pulled up to the house, I spotted my dad's car in the driveway. I walked up to the front door and opened it. I saw my dad sitting in the living room, staring right at me as if he'd been in that position for the last two days.

"WHERE IN THE FUCK HAVE YOU BEEN?!" he screamed, getting up from his chair and quickly moving toward me like an overweight panther.

"Listen, hold on," I said.

And then I launched into an elaborate lie about a school project and a birthday that made no sense before he cut me off.

"Mexico!! You went to fucking Mexico? They'll gut you like a pig, piss on your corpse, and then say 'Welcome to Mexico!'" he screamed. "You say you're going to fucking be somewhere, you fucking be there!" he added.

"I know, I know!" I hollered back in defense.

"No, you don't know! You don't know shit! Everyone is worried sick about you. I got your mother freaking out, then everybody else. I called the cops to look for you!"

"You called the cops?" I said.

"Yeah, I called the cops!"

"Well, shouldn't you call them and tell them you found me?"

My dad paused for a split second.

"They'll figure it out," he said, the tone in his voice changing.

I looked at him. He very rarely lied to me, and when he did, it was obvious.

"You didn't call the cops, did you?" I asked suspiciously.

"I called somebody," he replied.

"Was that somebody the cops?"

Silence fell over the room.

"No," he said, a little embarrassed. "But fuck you! I could have called the cops! I should have called them, but I figured you were just being dopey, and I'd have wasted their time!"

I realized I had somewhat disarmed him and should just cut my losses now and try to make things right. So I apologized profusely, explained that I had gotten caught up and completely forgotten about our date, and reaffirmed all the reasons why I was an idiot.

"Okay, okay, I get it, you don't have to keep listing reasons why you're a dumb shit," he said, interrupting my laundry list of self-insults.

He motioned me over to him. I cautiously approached. Then he grabbed me and gave me a big hug.

"You little shit," he said. "I can't wait till you have some kid and you got to worry about what happens to him. You never stop worrying about your children. It sucks. You watch what you stick your dick into, because this is your life, this bullshit right here."

He released me from the hug and grabbed a plastic grocery bag filled with chips.

"Grab that bottle of ketchup, we're late for the barbecue your uncle is throwing."

"I was going to meet Dan at the beach, actually," I said tentatively, hoping he would respect my Fourth of July plans.

"Shut the fuck up and grab the bag. You got some balls."

On Finding the Best Deal

"Man, you should have seen your mom tear that RadioShack manager a new asshole. I would venture to say she made a home inside his asshole. That will be the last time RadioShack tries to fuck with your mother."

On Nontraditional Entertainment

"There's something to be said for sitting around and drinking a beer while you watch your dog try to fuck a punching bag."

On the Baseball Steroids Scandal

"People are surprised Mark McGwire did steroids? Look at him! He looks like they should have him in a stall on display at the fair with some poor son of a bitch cleaning up his shit."

On My Decision to Try to Make It as a Hollywood Screenwriter

"It's like being on a merry-go-round, except the horse you're riding fucks you."

On Driving Through West Hollywood, Where
I Lived My First Year in L.A.

"There seem to be a lot of gay people there. . . . Oh please, as if that's what I meant by that. Trust me, none of them would ever want to fuck you anyway. They're gay, not blind."

On Being Lonely and Having Trouble Making Friends

"Have you tried going out to places, talking to people, making an effort? . . . Bullshit. Talking to someone in a Jiffy Lube waiting room is not making an effort."

On Internet Service

"I don't want it. . . . I understand what it does. . . . Yes, I do. And I don't give a shit if all of your friends have it. All of your friends have dopey fucking haircuts, too, but you don't see me running to my barber."

On Bragging

"I would simmer down a bit if I were you. . . . Well, for one, the only one who was impressed was the little girl sitting behind you, and for two, they don't exactly hand out Medals of fucking Honor for eating two Denny's breakfast plates in one sitting."

On Dealing with Loud Neighbors

"Have you told them it bothers you? . . . Are they bigger than you? . . . Are you afraid of getting your ass kicked? . . . Ah, okay, I probably should have asked that question first, woulda saved time. Yeah, you're just gonna have to deal with the noise, son."

At the End of the Day, at Least You Have Family

"So there you go. Your mother thinks you're handsome. This should be an exciting day for you."

A couple months after I graduated from college, I finally left my hometown of San Diego and moved to Los Angeles. I had studied film and television in college, specifically focusing on writing, and decided that I wanted to try my hand at becoming a screenwriter.

"Listen, it's gonna be tough, and you're gonna eat a lot of shit at first, but you just get past that, and you will succeed," was the advice my dad gave my brother Evan at the September dinner when we both announced our new professional goals. Evan had decided to embark on a career in scuba diving.

"Get ready for a fucking of biblical proportions," was the advice he gave me about twenty seconds later, after I shared my plan.

My dad believed in me, though, and supported my decision

completely. In fact, he supported me so much that, unprompted, he offered to pay my first three months of rent in L.A. to help me get on my feet.

"I figure, what's the fucking point in dying and leaving you money when you probably won't need it? Might as well give it to you now when you need the help. Plus, I plan on blowing most of it on stupid shit when I get senile," he explained.

I found a two-bedroom apartment in a small, ten-unit, white stucco building in West Hollywood. I shared it with a friend from college who was also trying to make it in the entertainment industry. The paint on our walls was peeling, and the carpet was covered in stains that would have made for a great *CSI* episode.

Even though I grew up two hours south, I had rarely ventured to Los Angeles. I soon learned that my dad wasn't totally off base when he said, "Los Angeles is like San Diego's older, uglier sister that has herpes."

Because I had barely any concept of what Los Angeles was like, I was met with a few surprises when I arrived—the first during my first night in the apartment. I learned that I shared a bedroom wall with our neighbors when I got into my old queen-size bed and heard the sounds of loud, passionate lovemaking coming through the thin stucco wall. I had never seen my neighbors before, but I had watched my fair share of porn, so immediately I envisioned a blond bombshell with huge breasts getting it on with a faceless man. My visual, paired with the live soundtrack, got me so excited that after listening for a few minutes I popped into my desktop computer the only porn DVD I owned and rubbed one out before dozing off. The next day, I walked out of my apartment just as my sexually active neighbors were strolling out of theirs.

"Hi, I'm Steven. This is my partner, Lucas," my neighbor said to me, introducing his larger male companion.

Hey, I'm Justin, I just jerked off last night to you and your boyfriend having sex, thinking you were a woman, and now I'm feeling fairly insecure about my sexuality, I thought.

I told them it was nice to meet them.

My roommate was an impressive person and a hard worker, and within two weeks of moving to L.A. she got an internship at a production company as well as a full-time job to pay the bills. Before I had fully unpacked my bags, she was working 90 to 100 hours a week, and I hardly ever saw her. I spent my days sending query letters to production companies, trying to get internships, while also looking for work pretty much every place I could think of. The only job I could find was delivering apartment guides to 7-Elevens in the greater Los Angeles area. I'd show up in the morning at a warehouse, load up the back of my truck with the thin realty booklets, and then struggle with directions for the next eight hours, trying to find out where exactly I was supposed to drop them off. It was like taking the worst tour of Los Angeles imaginable, and the job was only freelance, so it didn't even offer the opportunity to make much money.

I had only one real friend in L.A., my writing partner, Patrick, with whom I had directed my student film and written a screenplay for a feature film in college. Both were fairly poor attempts, but we had fun. We were learning and, most important, worked well together and had similar senses of humor. Patrick had lived in L.A. just a little longer than I had and was showing me the ropes as best he could. But except for him, the only people I saw on a regular basis were the transvestite prostitutes who hung out in front of my apartment complex. One of them approached me a few weeks into my stay, and part of me was actually excited by the prospect of having a conversation with someone new.

"Is this your car?" she asked, pointing to my white Ford Ranger.

"Yeah," I said.

"My girlfriend accidentally threw up on it last night, but I washed it off. Just wanted to say sorry," she said before walking away.

For the first time in my life, I was homesick. "How's it going up there?" my dad asked me over the phone when I called home after about a month to say hello.

"Oh, you know. Pretty good," I said, not wanting him to see what a sad sack I felt like.

"Bullshit, you're lying. I can tell by your voice."

"It's not going so great, Dad."

I told him everything that had been going on, just poured out all of the emotions that had been building up.

"From now on, when I ask you how you're doing, I appreciate you being open, but don't tell me stories about you jerking off to your gay neighbors," he said, laughing. "Listen, you've only been up there a month. This shit takes time. Steven Spielberg didn't become Steven Spielberg in a month. He was probably just some asshole who's a lot fucking uglier than you, I might add."

He talked to me for a few more minutes about the Padres and the

Chargers, how my brothers and my mom were doing, and afterward I felt a lot better. So I plugged away, and a couple months later I got a job waiting tables at a place called Crocodile Cafe in Old Town Pasadena. It was basically a lower-key T.G.I. Friday's. Landing the job was a minor victory, but my dad thought otherwise.

"Bullshit, you done good. It's hard to get a waiter job in L.A. All these fucking actors, they got all the jobs. Your mom and I are proud of you. We're gonna come up and take you out to celebrate," he said.

"That's really not necessary, Dad."

"Bullshit." (My dad loves the word *bullshit* and delivers it with many different inflections. This particular time, his delivery said to me, "This is not something you can argue against.")

My parents wanted me to feel good about myself, and they knew that I wasn't going to have a shot at being successful unless I did. I wasn't Charles Bukowski; my misery was not going to translate to literary genius and royalty checks. My dad ended the phone call with one emphatic sentence.

"I'm taking you to Lawry's Prime Beef!"

Lawry's is mostly known for its seasoned salt, which you can purchase in almost any large grocery store, but they also have a famous steak house, Lawry's The Prime Rib Restaurant, in Los Angeles, which my dad loves. Shortly after our phone call, he had my mom (who had broken him down and gotten Internet on her computer in the house) create an e-mail address for him just so he could send me an e-mail with a link to the Lawry's Web site. The subject heading was "Lawry's" and the body simply said, "This is fucking prime beef!" with the link to their menu.

The next Friday, my parents picked me up in my brother's Chevy Blazer, which he had left with them since venturing to Hawaii to start his scuba diving career.

"Who's ready for some fucking prime beef?!" Dad said as I stepped into the car.

Then he proceeded to ask me questions about my writing, life in Los Angeles, and pretty much anything else he could think of on the twenty-minute drive to the intersection of La Cienega and Wilshire boulevards, where the restaurant sat. I had invited Patrick, who met us in the restaurant's lobby. The four of us sat down at a table and as soon as we had our drinks, my dad called for a toast to me and Patrick.

"To you guys. For sticking your asses out on the line and going after it. And to Justin for getting a new job."

I never would have thought a person could so energetically toast a job that paid minimum wage, but my dad's pride was completely genuine.

The waitress who was covering our table was blond with big blue eyes. Even in the unflattering Lawry's waitress uniform, she looked very attractive. As usual, my dad went into full flirting mode. He started asking her every conceivable question about Lawry's history, the prime beef, the seasoned salts, and then moved on to questions about her personal life—where she lived (Hollywood), what she did (actress)—and so on. When my mother made the mistake of trying to order the only seafood dish on the menu, my dad used the opportunity to crack a joke.

"Aw, Joni, you're killing me. KILLING me. This is Lawry's. This is prime beef. You can't come here and order seafood," he said, a little too enthusiastically, to my mom. "Am I right, or am I right?" he added, gazing up at our waitress.

Though my dad likes to say he's not a flirt, his way with women is a big family joke. Whenever we call him on it, he replies with, "Oh please, I'm a married man. I'd never cheat on your mother, and she'd cut my nuts off anyway if I did, so there'd be no point in cheating. She's Italian, she'd do it."

In addition to loving women, my dad has always had a great affection for waiters and waitresses. He thinks they're hard workers who often get treated poorly by customers, so any time he eats out, he tips 30–40 percent, no matter what. I glanced at the bill and noticed it was around $220, which was definitely the most expensive dinner he had ever taken me to. We almost never went out to fancy meals, so I could tell this meant a lot to him. As I stared at the bill, I saw him jot down $80 for the tip.

Now, having worked in the restaurant industry for eight years— as a waiter for five of them—I can tell you that we operate the same way a stripper does: Give us money, and we'll pretend we like you. After our waitress saw the tip, she sashayed back to the table and began chatting us up even more. When my dad found out she was single, he pointed at me and said, "That one is single, too. He lives up here now. You two should get together." (Because if there's any indication that two people should begin having sexual intercourse, it's that they live in the same city.)

Ten minutes later, we finally got up from the table. My dad thanked each and every employee he saw on the way out as if he were walking offstage after winning an Oscar. Then he grabbed a toothpick from the dispenser at the hostess desk, popped it in his mouth, and strolled out the door. My parents and I bid farewell to Patrick, and when the valet brought our car around, my dad jumped in the driver's seat, my mom in the passenger's, and me in the back. After a few moments of silence, he looked at me in the rearview mirror and said, "That waitress, she was sweet on you. She was chatting you up for ten minutes."

"No, you gave her a huge tip, so she was being nice. You asked her to describe in-depth the beef preparation, and that took eight of those ten minutes," I replied.

"You don't know shit. I know when a woman is sweet on someone, and that girl was sweet on you."

Our argument escalated, with him insisting she liked me and me refusing to believe that, until finally it ended with my dad yelling, "Fine, she thought you were a jackass! You're right, I'm wrong!"

Silence filled the car for about fifteen seconds, until my mom turned around, looked me in the eye, smiled, and said, "I think you're handsome!"

"So there you go. Your mother thinks you're handsome. This should be an exciting day for you," my dad barked.

We rode the rest of the way home mostly in silence. A few times my dad pointed out landmarks he recognized from when he had lived in Los Angeles in the late sixties. We arrived at my apartment, and he parked the car on the street in front.

"You can just drop me off. You don't have to park," I said.

"Bullshit," he replied, jerking the emergency brake into place.

Both my parents got out of the car, and my mom gave me a big hug and told me how much she loved me and how proud of me she was. Then my dad grabbed me and enveloped me in his standard bear hug, which consisted of squeezing the life out of me while simultaneously patting my back with his right hand.

"Don't think you can't call us unless something big happens. Don't be one of those guys, because those calls, they take a little while to happen," he said.

"I know."

"You're trying. You're giving it a go. That's a big deal to me. You may not think things you do mean shit, but remember that they mean shit to me, okay?"

"I know."

"Yeah, you know everything. That's why you jerked off to your gay neighbors."

"Dad, we're right in front of their apartment."

He laughed, then gave me another hug.

"You always got us. We're family. We ain't going anywhere. Unless you go on a fucking killing spree or something."

"I would still love you, Justy. I would just want to know why you did it," my mom said earnestly, having gotten back into the car and rolled down her window.

My dad got back into the driver's seat and leaned over my mom to see out the passenger window.

"Remember. Family," he said. "Also, how do I get back to I-5? I hate this fucking city."

On Airlines' Alcohol Selection

"They serve Jim Beam on airplanes. Tastes like piss. You wouldn't be able to tell the difference, because you drink shit. I don't."

On Managing One's Bank Account

"Don't get mad at the overdraft charge.... No, no—see, there's your problem. You think of it as a penalty for taking out money you don't have, but instead, it might help you to think of it as a reminder that you're a dumb shit."

On Corporate Mascots

"Love this Mrs. Dash. The bitch can make spices.... Jesus, Joni, it's a joke. I was making a joke! Mrs. Dash isn't even real, damn it!"

On Understanding One's Place in the Food Chain

"Your mother made a batch of meatballs last night. Some are for you, some are for me, but more are for me. Remember that. More. Me."

On Birthdays

"Listen, I don't give a fuck if you forget my birthday. I don't need people reminding me I'm closer to death. But your mom, she still enjoys counting them down, so cancel your fucking plans and drive down here for her birthday party. . . . Fine, I'll let you know if she changes her mind and ceases to care about meaningless milestones."

On How to Tell When a Workout Is Complete

"I just did an hour on the gym machine. I'm sweaty, and I have to shit. Where's my fanny pack? This workout is over."

On Aging

"Mom and I saw a great movie last night. . . . No, I don't remember the name. It was about a guy or, no, wait—fuck. Getting old sucks.

On the Proper Amount of Enthusiasm

"You hear that? Your brother's engaged! . . . 'Yeah'? Did you just say 'yeah'?
What the fuck is that? . . . No, that's not gonna fucking cut it unless you say it
while you're doing a somersault or something."

Sometimes It's Nice When People You Love Need You

"Listen, the dog likes garlic salt, so I give him fucking garlic salt."

After having lived in Los Angeles for about a year, I decided that it would be cool to get a dog. Notice that I said "cool," not "a good idea" or "cool to think about." I wanted a dog and wasn't considering non-dog options.

When I was a kid, my family had a dog named Brownie, who I enjoyed playing with, particularly when my older brothers were no longer living at home. I loved that dogs just seemed to do whatever they wanted, whenever they wanted; it was a quality I admired. One time during a family dinner when I was around thirteen, I looked outside and Brownie was in the backyard, licking himself vigorously until he ejaculated on his own face. Then he lay down and went to sleep as if nothing had happened. Self-administering oral sex is not my cup of tea, but you have to hand it to him for his ruthless determination to enjoy himself.

A year out of college, I had a decent job waiting tables at an upscale Italian restaurant where I only needed to work about three days a week to make ends meet. I spent most of the rest of my time writing in my bedroom. I thought getting a dog might spice up my life a little bit.

"You can barely take care of yourself. Where are you gonna keep him?" my friend Dan asked.

"My apartment," I said.

"You don't have a yard. Where's he gonna go to the bathroom, or run around? Dogs need to run around. They can't just sit around an apartment."

"I'll get a small dog. If I was tiny, my apartment would seem huge, right?"

I knew my dad would probably have a similar response so I didn't tell him, or any of our family members who might leak the news to him. My roommate had grown up with dogs in her house and did not object. So I made a trip up to the pound in Lancaster, California, which is about fifty miles northeast of L.A., and scoured the narrow, cage-lined halls, passing dozens of sad and snarling faces in search of the perfect puppy.

"I want something that's gonna stay small," I said to the pound employee who was guiding me.

The worker assured me she'd help me find a small dog, and led me to a cage filled with six tiny brown puppies. I couldn't tell what kind of dogs they were; they just looked like mutts. I pointed out the smallest one, and a week later, after he had gotten his shots, I returned to the pound to pick him up. I named him Angus after Angus Young, the lead guitarist of AC/DC.

Very early on, I realized I might have made a huge mistake. Angus was a fun, loving dog, but he had an unbelievable amount of energy and suffered from serious abandonment issues. Every time I left him alone in the apartment, I'd return to find my living room carpet covered in dog crap. Evidently, he'd take a rebellious—or emotional—dump, then step in it and walk around the house like he was re-creating a Jackson Pollock painting. At first, I thought he did this because he had to empty his bowels, so I started taking him out to do his business right before I left. He'd go right away, but still, when I came back home after leaving him alone, his feces would be everywhere. I'd have to get out my cleaning supplies and go to town for an hour on the mess, just to make the apartment bearable. My roommate was a good sport, but she was quickly tiring of the situation.

About two months after I got Angus, I returned home to find that he had gotten into the cupboard where I kept his dog food. The door was open, and little pellets of dog food had spilled all over the kitchen floor. Normally, as soon as I walked through the front door Angus would greet me with a slobbering grin and wagging tail. This time I heard nothing. I turned toward the living room and saw him lying on the couch on his back, paws in the air, like a man who had been challenged to a pie-eating contest and had won in double overtime.

"Angus, nooooooo!" I intoned.

He rolled his distended belly toward me, then gave me a look that I had only ever received once in my life—from a sorority girl stumbling in front of my college apartment complex, right before she projectile-vomited on the ground. What happened next did not happen to her, fortunately.

I picked Angus up by the sides of his belly and, like a plastic IV bag whose hole had been stretched, a steady stream of diarrhea shot out of his butt onto the couch and floor. That was the final straw. The power of denial is strong, but seeing—and smelling—your furniture covered in fresh dog diarrhea is stronger. It was time to give Angus away.

But I loved him, so I wanted to give him to someone I would be able to visit on occasion, to check on him. My brothers and all of my friends immediately turned down my request to take Angus. That left one option: my parents. They had a big backyard, and Angus was growing at a ridiculously rapid rate. A dog that I was told would be no bigger than thirty pounds when fully grown weighed thirty-five pounds at only four months.

Angus was adorable, and I knew that the best strategy would be to casually show him to my parents before dropping the bomb on them. I wasn't worried about my mom; she was always easy to win over. My dad, of course, was a different story.

So, on a sunny Saturday morning in April, I drove down to San Diego with Angus on my lap, and walked into my parents' house unannounced, carrying him like an oversized baby.

"Awww, look at him, he's so cute!" my mom said, coming out from the kitchen, where she had been cooking, to pet him.

"That is a good-looking dog right there," my dad said, reaching over and rubbing his ears.

"Wait. Whose dog is this?" my mom asked, suddenly suspicious.

"Well, here's the thing," I said.

I went on to explain the whole scenario, fudging a few details to make me sound less impulsive and Angus like less of a handful.

"We can't take this dog. This is your responsibility—we can't just take a dog because you didn't think things through," my mom said, her tone increasingly annoyed with every word she spoke.

I was surprised and became worried because if my mom was reacting like this, I could only imagine what my dad was going to say. He was quiet for a few moments, and then he grabbed Angus and held him up.

"We can take care of him."

"Sam?" My mom was as surprised as I was.

"It's a dog. It's not like Justin knocked up some lady and he's walking in with a kid."

"Yeah, I didn't do that," I said, chuckling.

"You bet your fucking ass you didn't," my dad snapped, without an ounce of humor in his voice.

My dad took Angus outside, rubbed his belly, and set him down on the ground.

"This is your new home. Shit and piss where you like," he said to Angus.

I felt the way I did at age twenty-one when I gambled in Las Vegas for the first time and won a hundred dollars on my first slot machine pull: unsure about what had happened but confident that I should take off before my luck turned.

"Okay. Well, I better get going, you know. I've got work tomorrow, and it's a long drive, so. . . ."

And with that, I hurried down the driveway, got in my car, and drove back up to Los Angeles.

Every couple months or so, I'd head home, and each time, Angus would be larger. Eight months later, he was 105 pounds. He looked like Scooby-Doo on steroids.

"Dad, he's so . . . buff. What are you feeding him?" I asked, during a visit around Angus's first birthday.

"In the morning he gets a half pound of ground beef, half pound of potatoes, and two eggs, then I cook that together and put some garlic salt on it."

"Garlic salt? Like he wouldn't eat it if it didn't have garlic salt?"

"Listen, the dog likes garlic salt, so I give him fucking garlic salt."

"So he's eating, like, three thousand calories a day?"

"Well, probably more, since I give him that same meal at night, too."

"Jesus Christ, Dad. That's why he looks like a WWF wrestler."

My dad explained to me that he had tried lots of traditional dog foods, but that Angus liked human meals cooked for him best.

"Isn't that a lot of work? I mean, you're like his personal chef."

I followed my dad outside as he carried the bowl of food he had just prepared for Angus. The instant he smelled the meal, Angus jumped up in excitement and put his paws on my dad's chest like a long-lost lover.

"Okay, okay, take it easy, you crazy son of a bitch," my dad said. Turning to me, he added, "Yeah, it's a lot of work, but he's my friend."

I couldn't believe what I had just heard. Was my dad becoming sentimental in his old age?

"Wipe that stupid fucking look off your face. I ain't crazy. They're called 'man's best friend,' for chrissakes. It's not like I made that up."

I told him I was glad that Angus had become a good friend.

"You know, I was never really a dog person before this. I mean, Brownie was great, but he was your brother's dog. And I had lots of dogs on the farm, but they were work dogs. I guess with all you guys gone, and Mom working all the time, it's nice to have somebody around who depends on me. And who tears up my fucking rose garden—goddamn it, Angus," he said, turning and pointing toward the churned-up soil that had once hosted his red roses.

"He's just like you: He's a pain in my ass, but I love him. And he shits everywhere. Which is mostly why he's like you," he added with a smirk.

On Airport Pickup Duties

"My flight lands at nine-thirty on Sunday. . . . You want to watch what? What the fuck is *Mad Men*? I'm a mad man if you don't pick me the hell up."

On Built-Up Expectations

"Your brother brought his baby over this morning. He told me it could stand. It couldn't stand for shit. Just sat there. Big letdown."

On Canine Leisure Time

"The dog is not bored. It's not like he's waiting for me to give him a fucking Rubik's Cube. He's a goddamned dog."

On Talking Heads

"Do these announcers ever shut the fuck up? Don't ever say stuff just because you think you should. That's the definition of an asshole."

On Long-Winded Anecdotes

"You're like a tornado of bullshit right now. We'll talk again when your bullshit dies out over someone else's house."

On Today's Hairstyles

"Do people your age know how to comb their fucking hair? It looks like two squirrels crawled on their head and started fucking."

On Tailgating the Driver in Front of Me

"You sure do like to tailgate people. . . . Right, because it's real important you show up to the nothing you have to do on time."

On My Brother's Baby Being a Little Slow to Start Speaking

"The baby will talk when he talks, relax. It ain't like he knows the cure for cancer and just ain't spitting it out."

On the Right Time to Have Children

"It's never the right time to have kids, but it's always the right time for screwing. God's not a dumb shit. He knows how it works."

You Have to Listen, and Don't Ignore What You Hear

"Sometimes life leaves a hundred-dollar bill on your dresser, and you don't realize until later it's because it fucked you."

As I mentioned in the introduction to this book, it was a breakup with a girlfriend that landed me back at my parents' house at age twenty-eight. Our split hadn't been one of those overdramatic ones where we screamed and cursed each other's names, then I left with the slam of the door and a "go to hell!" I'd been through a couple breakups before, one of which ended with my ex saying, "Go fuck yourself, you stupid fuck." That was easy to get over; you don't stay up late at night hoping the woman who called you a stupid fuck comes back. In fact, none of my previous relationships ever felt that serious. But I had been with this girlfriend for three years, and I was sure that we were right for each other and had thought we would marry at some point.

When she decided to call it quits, it wasn't because of anything specific. Something that had been there before was now missing, and neither of us could figure out what. Our relationship just wasn't working. So when I moved into my parents' house, I was really down. I don't generally wear my emotions on my sleeve, but my dad could tell I was upset.

"Sometimes life leaves a hundred-dollar bill on your dresser, and you don't realize until later it's because it fucked you," he said, putting his hand on my shoulder while I was eating breakfast one morning about a week after I'd moved back home.

"It's okay. You don't have to try to cheer me up," I replied.

"Shit, I know that," he said. "But I figured I had to say something. Otherwise, just grabbing the cereal from you and leaving might seem a little callous." He chuckled, hoping to lighten the mood.

The next day I woke up at around six-thirty in the morning. Unable to go back to sleep, I groggily sauntered out into the living room in my boxer shorts. My dad was sitting at the dining room table eating Grape-Nuts and reading the paper.

"When'd you wake up?" I asked.

"Oh, I don't know, five maybe. Like usual."

"Jesus, that's early. Why do you wake up so early?" I said.

"Always have."

"But why? You're retired now. It makes no sense."

"Son, am I being interrogated here? I'm an early riser, what the fuck you want from me?" he said before resuming reading the paper.

After a few moments he put the paper down.

"Why are *you* up so early?"

I told him I had woken up and couldn't get back to sleep. He got up from his seat, walked into the kitchen, and poured me a cup of coffee.

"You want that bullshit you like in your coffee?" he asked, holding a mug filled with the dark black liquid.

"Creamer? Yes. I want creamer."

He set my coffee down on the table and went back to reading his paper. I poured myself a bowl of cereal, and we sat in silence for a few minutes. My mind was quickly consumed with thoughts of my girlfriend and all the good times we had had, like one of those cheesy montages in eighties movies, when the angsty protagonist envisions himself and his ex holding hands on the beach, feeding a small puppy, getting into some kind of zany wrestling match with whipped cream. I interrupted my cliché memories by saying aloud, "Ugh, I'm feeling pretty low about this whole thing."

"You just gotta try to put it out of your head," he said, folding the paper halfway down to look at me.

"I know, it's just hard. I mean, I still have stuff at her place. What am I gonna do about that? I still have a TV . . . ," I said.

"Fuck the TV. Leave the TV. Cut your ties."

"It's a fifteen-hundred-dollar TV," I insisted.

"Go get that fucking TV."

I wasn't sure what I was hoping to accomplish by having this conversation, but it wasn't making me feel better. So I went to take a shower, got dressed, and began working on my latest Maxim.com piece, which was, ironically, a flow chart detailing the differences between the male and female brain during an argument. I worked straight until twelve-thirty, when my dad came into the living room. He had his fanny pack on, which indicated he was ready to go somewhere.

"I'm buying you lunch. Put your flip-flops on and let's go."

I dragged myself off the couch, followed him outside, hopped in his car, and we headed down the hill to my favorite lunch spot, an Italian place near our house called Pizza Nova. We got a table outside in the sun that overlooked dozens of white clusters of sailboats and motorboats in the San Diego harbor. The waitress brought us a basket of garlic rolls and a pair of iced teas. My dad took a sip of his and looked up at me.

"You don't know shit about me."

"Um, okay," I said, a little confused.

"About my life. You don't know shit about it. Because I don't tell anybody."

It wasn't until he said it that I realized he was right. Sure, I knew the rough outline of my dad's biography: He grew up on a farm in Kentucky; served in Vietnam; had two sons with his first wife, who passed away from cancer shortly after having my brother Evan; married my mom nine years later and had me; and spent his career doing cancer research as a doctor of nuclear medicine. But that was it. Now that I was thinking about it, I realized he was probably the most private person I knew.

"When I was in my early twenties, I was head over heels for this woman. She was gorgeous. Just a real beauty. And full of life," he said between bites of a garlic roll.

Most of us like to assume, or wish, that our parents only had sex with each other, and only the necessary number of times it took to produce us and our siblings, so it was strange to hear my dad talk so highly about a woman other than my mother. He never had before, and I was intrigued.

"So me and her, we dated for a while. A long while. Then, one day, we got to talking, and I told her how much I loved her, and she looked at me and told me, 'I don't love you. I never will,'" he continued. "I'll have a sausage-and-pepperoni pizza with the salad," he said, turning to the waitress, who had been awkwardly standing next to our table waiting for my dad to finish his story so she could take our order.

I placed my order, and the waitress left.

"So what'd you do?" I asked.

"I told her I thought that I could change that. Maybe she didn't love me right now, but she would eventually."

"What'd she say?"

"She said okay. And we stayed together. And we fought. We fought a lot. And then I realized I had made a big mistake. She had given me her youth, and it was gone, and I didn't know how to get out of it. And then she got sick. And she was dying," he said, taking a deep breath, thinking for a moment, as if he were replaying something in his mind he hadn't thought of in a long time.

"So I made good with her, and I stuck by her. And then she died. And I felt horrible. Because I felt like here was this woman who didn't want to be with me, she told me that, and I ignored it. And she was spending the end of her life with someone she didn't love. And now she was gone. And part of me felt relieved that I was freed out of this relationship, and that made me feel so terrible, I couldn't deal with it."

My dad sat back in his wicker chair for a few quiet moments. The waitress arrived with our food, and he picked at his salad before looking up at me.

"People are always trying to tell you how they feel. Some of them say it outright, and some of them, they tell you with their actions. And you have to listen. I don't know what will happen with your lady friend. I think she's a nice person, and I hope you get what you want. But do me a favor: Listen, and don't ignore what you hear."

A few months later, I began writing this book. I sat down with family and friends, rehashing many different stories about me and my dad. We recalled things he said, and things they said, and we pieced together as best we could everything that's in these pages. As I was finishing up in December 2009, my dad called me one day while I was out buying groceries at Trader Joe's.

"Hey," he said.

"Hey, what's happening?" I asked.

"I know what your last chapter is," he said.

"Oh yeah?"

And then he told me he wanted this story to be the last chapter. I told him that this anecdote and the advice that accompanied it had meant a lot to me, but I realized how personal it was, and how private he was. I asked him why he wanted it to be the last chapter, and told him that the request seemed out of character for a guy who a month prior had told me that he'd consider pulling his shotgun on any reporter who came too close, asking questions about this book.

"Well, I figure this book is about you and me. I mean, I'm the star, but you're in it, too." He laughed. "And when I told you that story, you were hurting. So I guess I want people to know that maybe I'm not the warmest human being on the fucking planet, but I love the shit out of you. The story I told you, the reason I don't tell nobody is because I never had a reason to. You're a pretty together kid."

"Thanks, I appreci—"

"Don't get me wrong, you've got a big fucking mouth, and you ain't the prettiest to look at, but I love you, and I want people to know that when it comes down to it, I'd do things for my family that I wouldn't do for nobody else."

A week or so later I finished the book. I was at the end of an all-nighter and strolled into the living room, where my dad was eating breakfast and reading the paper.

"I'm done! I finished the book," I boasted.

"I cannot believe someone is going to publish something you wrote," he said.

"I know. Crazy, right?"

"You have never, ever in your life, had anything published. Ever. You've never had one goddamned word of yours published any-where!" he said, still in disbelief. (My dad has never counted my online writings "published"—or publishable.)

"I mean, not one fucking thing! Not a thing! And now YOU, you're going to have a book in stores and shit?! Jesus H. Christ. Un-fucking-believable. To think—"

"OKAY, I GET IT. I've never published anything, I'm the luckiest person on earth. I don't deserve it. I get it," I shouted.

"Oh shit, sorry, son, I didn't mean to bust your balls there. It's just, well, it's fucking unbelievable, that's all." He paused and offered me a seat on the couch next to him. "Congratulations, I'm proud of you. Have some Grape-Nuts."

He poured me a bowl and handed me the sports section. It was quiet for a few moments as we ate breakfast and read the paper.

"It's just, I'm having trouble wrapping my head around it," he said, looking up from his paper again and shaking his head. "I mean, they gave you money to do this. YOU. Amazing."

Acknowledgments

One of the best parts of writing this book was sitting down with my brothers, mom, and, of course, my dad, and remembering all these quotes and stories about our family. Without them, I never could have recalled the details that hopefully make this book an enjoyable one for people to read, and that really capture what my dad is like. Dan, Evan, José, Mom, and Dad, thank you.

I think any time you write about your life, you're never sure if it's going to be interesting or funny to anyone else, so thankfully I was lucky to have a few friends and colleagues help me along the way. Thanks to Amanda Schweizer, Cory Jones, Robert Chafino, Patrick Schumacker, Lindsay Goldenberg, Brian Warner, Dan Phin, Ryan Walter, George Collins, Andrew Fryer, Katie Deslondes, Kate Hamill, and Byrd Leavell.

I feel so fortunate to have been given the opportunity to write this book. As my dad said when I finished it, "Hopefully people give a fuck. Hopefully for you, not me."